Published by Remember Media Ltd in 2018. All rights reserved. No part of this publication may be reproduced or transmitted in any form or by any means, electronic or mechanical, including photocopy, recording or information storage without prior permission in writing from the publisher.

Editor Brian Nicholls
Written by Dennis Middleton
Published by Remember Media

Remember Media Limited, e-volve Business Centre, Cygnet Way,
Rainton Bridge South Business Park, DH4 5QY
www.remembermedia.co.uk

ISBN 978-0-9933710-3-5

A FAMILY TREASURE SHARED

My father, Dennis, joined the Territorial Army before the start of the Second World War because he knew war was coming. He told me he had never believed Chamberlain's claims of "peace in our time".

He chose to join the artillery. Memories of the First World War were fresh enough to dampen enthusiasm for the infantry! He went to war a few months later, telling his mother he would be back in a couple of years. In fact he was to be away for five years.

Dennis was posted to the Middle East and saw action in at least six major battles of the desert campaign. He was among the few to serve under Wavell in the early days and under Monty after that. He was at the siege of Tobruk from beginning to end. His best friend was killed and he himself was captured... only to be freed by our army six days later. There was plenty of action.

However, this is not a military story. It's the story of an ordinary young man of 21 who experienced extraordinary times. It tells of jokes and japes, of horror and of comradeship. It is a straightforward and unsentimental tale, intelligent and gently humorous, just like my father.

After the war he returned to work for Barclays Bank and had a conventional, but successful, career ending up as a senior manager. After his retirement, he spent more than two decades happily travelling the world with my mother, Vivienne, up to his death at 87 in 2005.

My father rarely mentioned the war despite the requests for stories from my brother Nicholas and me. However, in the mid-1990s he handwrote this memoir as a record for himself and our family.

I publish it now to share his story. His were experiences shared by many of his generation - experiences my generation has been spared - and experiences I hope and pray my children will be spared, too.

Jeremy Middleton

CONTENTS

1.	**LEAVING HOME** …AND EASY LIVING ON TWO BOB A DAY	7
2.	**SORELY TROUBLED** THE AGONY OF DESERT LIVING	13
3.	**TAKING OF THE 5,000** NO CASUALTIES, PLENTY OF FUN	25
4.	**LETTER TO A WIFE** ON THE DEATH OF A DEAR FRIEND	33
5.	**COMMANDERS DOWN** …BREAKOUT EXACTS ITS PRICE	41
6.	**FORAY FOR FAROUK** OUR GUNS TRAIN ON HIS PALACE	49
7.	**MONTY MOVES IN** …AND WE LEAD OUR GUNS A DANCE	57
8.	**BOOKS AND BEDOUINS** …AND MENACING MINES	67
9.	**DIRECTION AT LAST** MASTERING THE PANZERS	75
10.	**TAKEN PRISONER** …AND CUT ADRIFT	81
11.	**A TIME TO INDULGE** …COMING TO TERMS WITH PEACE	89
12.	**SEEING THE SIGHTS** …AND PARADING WITH A FOUR-LEGGED FRIEND	99
13.	**ONWARD TO ITALY** …AND EMBARRASSING BREAKFAST	107
14.	**LADY IN THE LEGION** …A MEMORABLE DINNER GUEST	111
15.	**AMAZING ENCOUNTER** …BROTHER PETER, OUT OF NOWHERE	117
16.	**STAGE DOOR JOHNNY** …FOR GOSSIP, NOT THE GIRL	123
17.	**A NATIONAL DILEMMA** TO FRATERNISE OR NOT?	127
18.	**AMONG THE ARISTOCRACY** …SURVIVORS OF CONFLICT	133
19.	**SINKING LOVE** HOW THE SEA COOLS PASSIONS	141
20.	**RETURN TO EGYPT**	151
HUSSAR MAP LEGEND		156
SEVEN GREAT ESCAPES		159

1939
CHAPTER 1

LEAVING HOME
...AND EASY LIVING ON TWO BOB A DAY

LEAVING HOME ...AND EASY LIVING ON TWO BOB A DAY

I celebrated my 21st birthday by joining the Territorial Army, little knowing what would follow. It was on the 23rd of April 1939. I had wanted to do so all the previous year, but had been reluctant to give up a week of my previous annual fortnight's holiday; the bank allowed members of the TA only one week additional leave towards their two weeks' call-up.

I was sworn in at the Drill Hall on Derby Road, Nottingham, having chosen to enlist as a gunner in the South Notts Hussars, otherwise the 107th Regiment, Royal Horse Artillery. To my disappointment, nobody offered me the King's Shilling. The following Saturday I had a birthday party of a meal at home for a dozen or so of my friends, followed by a visit to the Theatre Royal. What we saw I cannot recall, but do remember I took some pride in announcing I was now Gunner Middleton. I was glad I had been able to choose for myself the unit in which I would serve in the war, which we all (all the young at any rate) knew was coming. I was from the beginning in 425 Battery, B Troop.

During the next few months the training I received was sketchy in the extreme, owing to the vast increase in numbers over a short time, and the lack of equipment. We were still equipped with First World War 18 pounder guns with iron tyres, and although I did some gun drill I soon found myself as a trainee driver. I enjoyed it when I got the chance to drive a 15 cwt truck, but we had very little transport. Indeed there seemed to have been a shortage of battle dress too, and I was issued with a service dress jacket of First World War style, which in fact looked rather smart with RHA ball buttons well polished.

June saw us off to camp at Redesdale in Northumberland. I, and some of my friends were nominated as "spare drivers" so we designated ourselves as members of the RCSD - the Royal Corps of Spare Drivers. I shared a bell tent with, I think, five men, who formed the basis of friendships lasting long afterwards in the desert. I should say, of course, I was a Driver I/C which meant "Internal Combustion"! This seemed a ridiculous designation at the time. But it was not long since the regiment had been full of horsed drivers pulling the guns.

The food was appalling. I particularly remembered having a mutton stew, almost entirely large chunks of fat, for breakfast. Yet nobody dared complain to the orderly officer. On the middle Saturday of camp we had a leave truck into Newcastle, the nearest English civilisation, 40 miles away. Once there, we found little to do bar go in to the pub which, needless to say, we all did. It was interesting that complete strangers came up and shook us by the hand in the street. I was reminded of Kipling's "it's thank you, Mr Atkins, when the band begins to play".

One day, unloading 18 pounder ammunition into an underground store, I dropped one of the heavy boxes. I jumped back a couple of feet in alarm, and for that I was the butt of jokes for some minutes. First, there was no danger whatever of the ammo exploding, but if it had the dump would have gone up and nothing would have been left alive within a hundred yards!

Over the next two months the prospect of war became more and more certain. At 2pm

1939, Redesdale camp

on Friday, 1st September I was sitting at my book-keeping machine in Barclays, St Peter's Gate, when staff returning after lunch came in excitedly to say that members of the TA were being asked on the wireless to report to their units. I rose from my machine, said a quick goodbye and left for home to put on my uniform and collect my kit. Another office colleague in the TA left too, but was never to return.

Along with swarms of others I reported to the drill hall. Our battery sergeant major, BSM Sykes, was a corporation bus driver, and for days he had been taking his loaded bus to the drill hall to ask if there was any news. Now the officer who received the orders for embodiment chased the BSM's bus in his car, and without further ado the loaded bus was driven to the depot, where BSM Sykes jumped into the car and was first in at the drill hall.

My battery, 425, was billeted in William Hollins factory along a cul-de-sac at the bottom of Derby Road. We slept on paliasses (straw mattresses) on the floor, very close together, and I made the mistake of picking a place against the wall near the exit door. The mistake lay in my being on the route to the lavatories, so anybody who had been on the beer was liable to stumble over me when he went out in the middle of the night, or worse, to throw up over me. No-one did, but I used to listen in the dark with trepidation to the approaching, unsteady footsteps.

We were there three weeks, during which I recall few military activities. An 18-pounder was delivered to Victoria Station, from where, since transport was lacking, we had to drag it up to the top of Derby Road by simple manpower. The first task was to get it up the ramp from the siding to Parliament Street, and it seemed particularly heavy up the slope of Derby Road, just beyond Chapel Bar. We tried it with drag ropes, we tried it without drag ropes, but we proved a poor substitute for a normal 30cwt gun-tower. However, we triumphantly reached the drill hall in the end.

On one occasion I was detailed to take charge of a prisoner under close arrest, and to march him down Derby Road from the drill hall to Hollins factory to feed. This I did, rifle at the slope, watched by many curious eyes.

I rose from my machine, said a quick goodbye and left for home to put on my uniform and collect my kit. Another office colleague in the TA left too, but was never to return.

One evening too I was on guard outside the drill hall, where there were, as usual, a few girls hanging about. One would have been in trouble for talking while on guard in a public place of this nature. So when a couple of girls started to chat and giggle I would come smartly to attention, slope arms, and march up to the other end of my beat. In the first three weeks of war, one acted in as military a manner as possible - a viewpoint which was not to last.

Before the end of September the regiment had moved to Rillington, near Malton in Yorkshire, where I was billeted on the upper floor of a very small cow shed, which just held eight palliasses side by side. It would never have passed health regulations. The communal latrines effectively inhibited me so that I suffered permanent constipation, relieved only when we went for a good meal at the local inn on Saturdays, and more importantly were able to use their WC. In early October the weather was pleasant, and a relaxing way of spending the afternoons was to go on map reading instructions with BSM Sykes. We would drive to a nearby range of hills and sit on the grass in the afternoon sun, while we were initiated into the mysteries of "reference bushy-topped tree, eight degrees, 2 o'clock…"

From 1st September I had struck up a close friendship with Philip Collihole, which would last until he was killed at Tobruk. It is only such friendships which make war tolerable, and we were linked by a common sense of humour. Phil was some six years older than I, and a salesman with W&T Avery, the weighing machine manufacturer. He came from Bristol and was a bachelor then.

Our next move was to Wragby, in Lincolnshire, by train. That was on 6th November. We were billeted in Halton Hall, two and a half miles away, and as we moved into frosty weather in December, washing outdoors in the yard in the darkness of early morning became something of an ordeal. Not that we washed a lot; we relied upon a weekly visit for a bath to the home of Margaret Milburn in Wragby, with whom someone had struck up a friendship. Physical training at 7am in the darkness was something of an easy ride, because no-one could see whether you were exerting yourself or not, although it was far too cold to relax for long. The vehicles we had, both civilian vans and army trucks, took a lot of starting when one went out at 6am to driving duty; it was invariably necessary to crank them, often for several minutes, to loosen up the oil.

I found I lived easily on my 10p-equivalent-today pay of 2/- a day (less deductions for cleaning materials etc). All one had to spend it on was the occasional visit to the pub in the next village and a Saturday trip into Lincoln. This was achieved by walking the two and a half miles to Wragby, then hitching a lift on a lorry for the next 11 miles. Phil and I visited

From 1st September I had struck up a close friendship with Philip Collihole, which would last until he was killed at Tobruk.

the cathedral at Lincoln, and I had a tailor make me a pair of army breeches, which together with my service dress jacket constituted the proper Royal Horse Artillery walking out dress – not forgetting my spurs! It afforded me a good deal of innocent amusement, but unfortunately I was only able to wear it two or three times since, in a few weeks, we were to have left the country.

Dowson Brown, from the Westminster Bank, installed his girlfriend Margaret in lodgings locally and told the proprietress that she was his wife. He paid regular conjugal visits, and we all approved this piece of enterprise, long before the days of any permissiveness. Dow, years afterwards, used to dine out on the story that he was the only bank manager who had been thrashed by the Governor of the Bank of England; so he had, when in the fourth form at high school by the head boy, then Gordon Richardson, who was Governor of the Bank in the 1970s.

A rumour went round: we were going abroad. We took in a reinforcement of militiamen and parted with all our under-19s to the Second Line Regiment, which would serve at home. By Christmas everybody had their embarkation leave and Phil married his fiancée, who was secretary to Richard Dimbleby, then an unknown at the BBC Bristol. When I left home I told my mother not to expect me back for a couple of years. I was only trying to dampen false hopes, but she wept. It would be five years before I returned.

On Boxing Day the advance party set out, nobody knew where. Old soldiers said it was sure to be Palestine, where the regiment had fought in 1914-18. Shortly before we left we had a regimental church parade, after which we were addressed by the honorary colonel, old Sir Lancelot Rolleston, then aged over 90. The parade was held in thick fog and frost and he appeared in service dress and without a coat for his last address to his regiment. He had joined the SNH in 1868!

When I left home I told my mother not to expect me back for a couple of years. I was only trying to dampen false hopes, but she wept. It would be five years before I returned.

1940
CHAPTER 2

SORELY TROUBLED
THE AGONY OF DESERT LIVING

The regiment was ordered to move at full trooping scale, which meant even gunners took two kit bags each. When we marched off from Halton each man had to carry one kit bag on his shoulder and his pack on his back. Fortunately we had the band in front of us but, even so, by the time we reached Wragby our marching presented a distinctly unmilitary appearance owing to the weight we were carrying. Only now did we know we were bound for Palestine. It was 18th January 1940 when we left Wragby station and travelled from Southampton via the sea transport Maid of Orleans. We then crossed France by train to Marseilles. It was bitterly cold, and the rail journey took two whole days. At Marseilles we embarked on the SS Dilwara, then the embarkation officer changed his mind and we all disembarked again. Finally, we were settled on the troop ship Devonshire, on which we spent the next eight days, sleeping and eating on the mess decks. In the morning hammocks were stowed and mess tables set up.

In the evening the process was reversed. It was not particularly easy to get out of a hammock at night, but if one did the sight of a hundred hammocks of sleeping men slowly swinging to and fro in the half darkness was unforgettable.

On board this ship I first came across the game of Crown and Anchor, which was strictly illegal in army terms. It grew dark early in the Med in January, and after tea crowds of men would congregate on the after deck, where about eight old sweats were each running a Crown and Anchor game lit by a single candle. There was a folding board bearing six symbols: ace, king, queen, jack, crown and anchor, on any of which one could bet. What the odds were I cannot remember. A friend, Pat Bland who, in civilian life, was a stockbroker, pursued a policy of betting on the anchor and doubling his stake every time he lost. After all, it was bound to come up on the dice some time, wasn't it! It didn't, and Pat lost six pounds which, when one was paid 14 old shillings a week represented a lot of money. It took him weeks to recover his finances, and I have never forgotten that doubling up is suicidal. The games would be at their height, amid cries from the operators of "any more for the dinky di?", "you can't pick it up if you don't lay it down", and the like. Suddenly there would be a warning cry from the top of the companionway of "orderly officer!" In one swift moment candles were blown out; boards, dice and money swept up and concealed; and there was nothing to be seen but soldiers quietly taking in the evening air. I always felt the officer moved very slowly to allow all this to be done; he knew very well what was going on. He would give us a polite "good evening", to which we all responded, and then would depart, and out would come the candles again.

The mess decks were stuffy at night, so one night Phil and I took our blankets up and slept under the sky on the bare deck. We did not repeat the experience; the Med in January is far from warm. One morning we woke to a brilliant sun and, going on deck, we saw before us the port of Haifa beneath Mount Carmel, my first sight of the East. When we disembarked, Arabs on the quay were selling oranges at a piastre a piece (100

= 1 pound), beautiful Jaffa oranges which we eagerly bought. A week or two later we were buying them at 12 for a piastre - or an akker, we always called it.

We went straight to Sarafand camp where it poured with rain and was deep in mud for the fortnight we were there. We then moved to a new camp at Gedera, which was little drier, although it quickly improved.

By March we were often swimming off what was known to be a most dangerous stretch of coast. By now my legs were covered in sores, the result of mosquito bites which had gone septic. I had to report to the medical orderly's room twice a day for fresh dressings, which was not particularly comfortable since the medical orderly, Harry Day, was not the gentlest of men. The medical officer, Dr Finnegan, was an Irishman who drank like a fish. He was, I believe, an excellent active service medical officer, but he failed entirely to achieve any improvement

> **We had to be back in camp by 6pm, curfew time, and sectors of both the Arab and Jewish populations were doing their best to kill the British.**

in my desert sores and I suffered with them for many months. Fortunately, when we reached Egypt, they seemed to clear up of their own accord.

We were only two miles from the Arab village of El Mughar, the scene of one of the South Notts 1914-18 Battle Honours. One Saturday we walked to this mud-built village perched on a hill and wandered around it, far more primitive then than today's Arab villages.

At the end of March we moved again, to Hadera, then a small Jewish village a mile from the sea north of Tel-Aviv. Only later would Tel Aviv become a large resort featuring on package tours. Then I used to enjoy wandering into the only village cafe to play my favourite record on the gramophone, My Heart Belongs to Daddy. We used to work from early morning until dinner time, then parade again from 4 till 6 pm, so that every afternoon was free. Every day in the sun we would walk, dozens of us, over the maquis covered low cliffs to the sea for two hours of sunbathing and swimming in the invigorating breakers. We rapidly turned a deep, dark brown colour all over, since we had no swimming trunks and were naked.

I had very few expeditions from Gedera and Hadera. We had to be back in camp by 6pm, curfew time, and sectors of both the Arab and Jewish populations were doing their best to kill the British. At one time we had to carry arms whenever leaving the camp, and I remember the difficulty of visiting the cinema in Rebovet and passing along the row to a vacant seat knocking everybody on the knees with my rifle. Unfortunately one was unable to have social contact with any of the Jewish population, which I would have liked, as I was trying to learn Hebrew. The only exception was the friendly little man at the gate who sold the English language Palestine Post, which we read regularly.

Tel Aviv, we went to several times by coach. A large modern city, there was little to

SORELY TROUBLED THE AGONY OF DESERT LIVING

Above: 1940, Hadera
Below: 1940, Hadera, Frank Bush, John Walker, Ted Coup, Dennis G Middleton (DGM), Bert Hayward

Above: 1940, Hadera, Bert Hayward, Ted Coup, DGM
Below: 1940, Hadera, Bert Hayward, DGM, Dow Brown, Geoff Douglas, unknown, Frank Bush

Left: 1940, Hadera, Phil Collihole

Right: 1940, Hadera, Charles Westlake, Phil Collihole, Bill Brameld

do bar sit in a cafe or go to the cinema. However, on one occasion I went off by myself to neighbouring Jaffa, which was completely Arab and completely devoid of British soldiery. There I entered a cafe and asked for a coffee and a nargileh (hookah). The hookah was brought alight and I endeavoured to master the technique of smoking it - not as easy as it looks. Either I smoked it gently, and it tended to go out, or I drew strongly on it and felt dizzy. The tobacco in the bowl was nothing like ours, and I have often wondered since whether it was indeed tobacco, or whether it was mixed with hashish or the like.

Another time four of us went to Haifa. Dow Brown, the battery clerk, had bought a large American car for £80, and parked it outside the battery office tent. We drove it to Haifa, but were somewhat late in leaving, so were still driving back after the curfew hour of 6pm, by which time the roads were utterly empty. We were conscious the car already had bullet holes in the wing, and we felt we might receive some more. But we returned uneventfully.

Best was the occasional coach trip to Jerusalem, across the fertile plain covered in orange groves, over the mountains, and down a hairpin-twisting road to the city lying at 2,500 feet. I saw the Church of the Holy Sepulchre, the Old City, the Wailing Wall, and the Garden of Gethsemane. We drove to Bethlehem a few miles away, and entered the

Church of the Nativity through its single, low, narrow doorway under which one had to stoop. Down a flight of stairs was the cave, and a virgin in a glass case, the interior of which was a foot deep in jewels. On one occasion we had an introduction through Phil's wife to some BBC staff at 168, Street of All The Prophets, a lovely old Arab house with a huge domed living room.

Most of the time was spent in quite intensive training. Although I still did some diving I was now training as a signaller but, regrettably, Phil Collihole and I treated the whole business of soldiery pretty flippantly, which culminated in an occasion when a night exercise was suddenly called at 10pm one night. Phil and I decided that since we had no vehicles to drive and no signalling function, no-one would miss us if we didn't go. We felt slightly uneasy when we woke in the morning to find the camp virtually deserted, and the regiment did not return from the exercise until the end of the day. We then found ourselves on a charge and up before our troop commander the following morning. "Hats off, quick march, left right, left right, halt!" We pitched him some yarn to explain our absence, but it was pretty unconvincing and we got off light with seven days confined to barracks. We also had a

We then found ourselves on a charge and up before our troop commander the following morning. "Hats off, quick march, left right, left right, halt!"

1940, Palestine, DGM, Phil Collihole, Gabb, Bob Foulds, Wortley, Geoff Chambers

SORELY TROUBLED THE AGONY OF DESERT LIVING

1940, Church of the Holy Sepulchre

1940, Bethlehem, Church of the Nativity

1940, Garden of Gethsemane

Lancer regiments kept their horses for some time, the last to lose them being, I believe, the Royal Scots Greys some two years later. Since we were Royal Horse Artillery we did not use infantry bugles but cavalry trumpets, and at Hadera they were well and truly used. An orderly trumpeter sounded calls for reveille, meals, parades, retreat and last post. I loved it, particularly retreat, sounded at sunset. Whenever it sounded one had to stand rigidly still and to attention, wherever one was, as the flag was lowered in the Mediterranean sunset. The sound remained tremendously evocative to me decades later.

Learning to become a signaller was talking to, the gist of which was that we were taking the Army too casually, not seriously enough, that we were potential non-commissioned officers, and must pull our socks up. Potential NCOs, we thought, very well, we will reform.

Since before the war the regiment had been part of the 1st Cavalry Division, and the unit's horses now arrived. I could hardly believe my eyes when I saw the horse lines – officers and NCOs were to be mounted – and I realised it was actually intended they should be used in action. In fact they never were, and were left behind when we departed from Palestine a month or two later. Around this time the cavalry units began to change over to armour, but many famous Hussar and

1940, Garden of Gethsemane

SORELY TROUBLED THE AGONY OF DESERT LIVING

Left: 1940, Beersheba, empire builder Bush
Below: 1940, Beersheba, camel races

Above: 1940, cafe in Beersheba

interesting and I felt it called for more individual skills than being a member of a gun team. The communication methods we used were all pretty much 1914-18, and an efficient knowledge of Morse code was essential. We had telephones, signal lamps, semaphore, Morse flat, heliograph and wireless. But in the end, when it came to action, only telephone and wireless were used. Helio was particularly skilled and satisfying, and can be used over long distances in the bright Middle Eastern sun. The signallers at regimental headquarters succeeded in transmitting from the camp to the hills 20 miles away. We also practised

Below: 1940, the well

Above: 1940, Ramleh cemetery

using climbing irons to lay overhead telephone wires. This was in the Rothschild Forest, a eucalyptus wood adjoining the camp. But it proved unsatisfactory since the irons would not grip properly the soft gum wood, which tore away.

At the end of April we moved temporarily to a firing camp at Asluj in the Negev, 80 miles beyond Gaza and south of Beersheba. It was pure desert then, very hilly and sandy, though no doubt it is now irrigated and fertile. The temperature remained at a steady 95 degrees in the shade. I learned to drive through soft sand and to change gear on a Morris pick-up truck without using the clutch. We had many shoots, and I also learned something of the difficult work of an observation post assistant. We shared the camp with an Australian Field Regiment recruited, among other ways, from Aussie prisons. It was an eye opener to visit the NAAFI tent in the evening and stand ankle deep in empty beer cans while crowds of Aussies played two-up for what seemed to us enormous sums.

In time off at the weekend we visited the stables of the Arab Camel Corps at Asluj, and went to Beersheba to the camel races, a great event where Arabs from vast distances wagered large sums on their Mahari, white racing camels. I saw the great well, some 15 feet across and immensely deep, with a donkey constantly circling it and drawing water. We were told that it was a well which Isaac dug, referred to in Genesis 26, and I am quite prepared to believe it.

We fired three shots over his grave and, never having rehearsed, did it very raggedly. I have always felt guilty about it.

At Asluj Bob Poulson was seized with appendicitis. He concealed his pain too long, and by the time he was rushed to hospital he had developed peritonitis and died. He was buried in Ramleh cemetery with military honours. The regimental trumpeters sounded the last post, and Bob Foulds and I were members of a firing party. We fired three shots over his grave and, never having rehearsed, did it very raggedly. I have always felt guilty about it.

We returned to Hadera 18th May and almost immediately heard of Italy's entry into the war. We were brought up to strength in guns at the expense of other yeomanry regiments and on 23rd June we entrained for Egypt, although in true army style nobody knew where.

1940
CHAPTER 3

TAKING OF THE 5,000
NO CASUALTIES, PLENTY OF FUN

At Tanta, where the train briefly halted, Egyptians on the platform sold "eggs and bread", and very good they were too. But the train started without warning, and half of 426 Battery were left behind, a state of affairs only remedied by the major and the BSM clambering from the first coach to the tender and then onto the engine, to stop the train in true wild west style. Together with another man at about this point on the journey, I got on the foot plate and, having previously lowered a few beers, decided it would be a good idea to sound the whistle a few times. I'm afraid the driver and fireman felt pretty helpless to stop us, but they smiled bravely and ultimately we gave up and seized the opportunity of the next halt to nip back to our carriage.

We seemed to travel westwards up the empty desert interminably, although in reality it was only about 200 miles. Ultimately, on arrival we found our destination was Mersa Matruh. In peacetime it must have been a delightful spot, although already the white-walled little town was largely destroyed by bombing. Its main feature was a beautiful oval lagoon in which Cleopatra reputedly bathed. It was a quite unique blue colour, and surrounded by low red cliffs and white sand, and it emptied into a great salt lake on which we had the use of a felucca. Since not many men knew how to sail, it was not difficult to get hold of it in the afternoons, when, for some months we did not work owing to the great heat, and there was always a good breeze.

Matruh was the defensive position to which our Army would fall back if necessary, and our guns were situated in pits with deep dugouts for command posts. Nevertheless, my main memory is of digging new gun pits and suchlike, which we did for months on end, broken only by the daily air raids. The routine was reveille at 6am and gunfire (cup of tea) at 8am. Breakfast followed by more digging until about 12.30. Afternoons were free, and usually meant a bathing party, until work started again at 4pm until 6-6.30. In August the free afternoons were cut out and we dug all day, but I received a personal insight into the philosophy of the British workman. We worked wearing only shorts, in temperatures of up to over 100 degrees, without hats, and no-one suffered from heat stroke that I heard of.

We had, of course, gradually accustomed ourselves to ever increasing heat from March onwards and by this time were nearly black in colour from head to foot (owing to bathing naked), a colour that was not actually very

My main memory is of digging new gun pits and suchlike, which we did for months on end, broken only by the daily air raids.

attractive. Thinking back, I remember that when the rear party from England joined us in Palestine they were so pale that I genuinely felt they must be ill. At last my legs covered in sores cured of their own accord, although everyone, of course, always had a few sores whenever one was in the desert.

For the first three weeks in Matruh I was

Below: 1940, Mersa Matruh, Ted Coup, DGM, Frank Bush
Right: 1940, the lake at Mersa Matruh
Bottom: 1940, Mersa Matruh

put in charge of the canteen at Rear Wagon Lines. Every morning I would take a truck to the NAAFI supply depot to stock up with supplies, and every evening my tent would open from 6pm until I got tired about 11pm, selling cigarettes, chocolates and beer. Basically, I was running a pub, an interesting experience, but it was seven days a week and I was glad when I moved to other duties.

There were disadvantages, sandstorms every few days, daily bombing, and hundreds of fleas in any dugout. As for bombing, one day I found myself with my truck miles from

Leave started in August, and the lucky ones came back with marvellous tales of the Happy Moon Hotel, apparently staffed by compliant girls.

our lines and caught in a raid. It was in an area occupied by Jewish pioneers, and when it was over much wailing announced that a slit trench had caved in where it was thought a Jewish soldier sheltered. We dug and soon revealed a head and pulled him out. None of the Jews appeared to have a clue as to what to do, so we put him in the back of my truck and I drove off as fast as I could in a direction I vaguely recalled having seen the garrison hospital. Fortunately my sense of direction ultimately proved correct, and I hauled him over to the medical staff. He was, as I had thought, dead – the first casualty I saw.

Our battery commander, Peter Birkin, was a tremendous character, an endless source of gossip to us gunners. He was a homosexual, but an excellent soldier. He was a keen rugby player with very broad shoulders and a narrow waist and large ginger moustache. He had a marked stammer. The Birkins were prominent in the South Notts: his father had commanded a battery in the 1914-18 war, and there were two other Birkins in the regiment now, Garry and Ivor. Ivor apparently had a game leg, but that had not stopped him. Pete had a habit of saying he wished to visit the observation post at dusk, to view the targets at dusk and dawn. He would nominate someone to go with him, sometimes a driver, sometimes an observation post assistant: whoever it was, was unmercifully ribbed as a subject for seduction, though I doubt if any one played Pete's game.

Leave started in August, and the lucky ones came back with marvellous tales of the Happy Moon Hotel, apparently staffed by compliant girls. My fun came in November, the first leave for nearly a year. Before taking it, we had a pay parade, and I asked for £100 (the equivalent of £6,000 today). The paying officer was most reluctant to give it to me: it represented five months' pay, since we had been in the desert for that time, and it was an enormous amount. However, I explained that I preferred to put my money in a bank rather than leave it to the tender mercies of the Army, so I got it. As soon as I got to Cairo I marched in the National Bank of Egypt and opened a current account. There it stayed until I came to the Officer Cadet Training Unit over a year later.

The cookhouse in those days operated with Soyer stoves. These were invented by

1940, December, DGM, Cairo Leave Middle East Force

Alexis Soyer in charge of Army catering during the Crimean War, so it was judged that in some ways the Army had not changed in 100 years. On the other hand, it may show that it is a very good design for field use.

I went to Cairo for a week with Phil Collihole, and we were not allocated to the Happy Moon (I think the Army had found out about that one) but to Jelley's. This was a hotel for the troops, with adequate NAAFI type food, and it was a great experience to have one's first bath for nearly a year. Mrs Seely the colonel's wife had followed her husband out to Egypt and started a club for the British soldiery, to which all the South Notts naturally gravitated. I met her years after the war when she was Lady Graham, and she was delighted to see someone who had known the club.

We were able to fill our time quite pleasantly, for there were plenty of interesting things to do – the Pyramids, by train and a camel ride; the Citadel; the Nile. There was also an excellent zoo where we saw two giant turtles interminably mating, and where a keeper, to entertain us, fed a live mouse to a large snake. The old bazaar at the Muski was fascinating: little boys who looked no more than eight making gold and silver filigree jewellery, eastern perfumes, donkeys pushing down crowded alleyways. In the evenings there were many cinemas showing English films and other ranks' night clubs, where one saw a series of belly dancers and stood drinks to taxi-drivers. The cafes which were open to the troops sold only NAAFI type food, permutations of egg, chips, bacon, sausage and tomato. Phil and I longed for a really good meal and at last found one in a nice restaurant open to all ranks, where we had a wonderful Chicken au King. One evening in a cafe we struck up a friendship with three Poles – mature, educated men in their thirties at least, one of whom had been a judge. When we parted I felt deeply impressed by their determination to leave their own country and make their way to Egypt to volunteer to fight as privates. In any other army they would have been officers, but many Polish ex-officers in the Middle East fought as other ranks.

We could not leave Cairo without a visit to have a look at the Berka – Sharia Wagh-el-Berka, the brothel street. We entered one. The ground floor was just an empty stone-flagged entrance hall, with stairs leading off, and round the first bend in the stairs we came across a queue of men stretching up the stairs and along a corridor, off which were the girls' rooms. The girls were of all colours, mostly pretty dark, and the few I saw looked incredibly unattractive. As for Madame, her raddled appearance was positively depressing, and after one long look we fled, our curiosity satisfied. These brothels were invariably crowded and were strictly under military control until Montgomery's arrival in 1942, when they were closed on his order. The price was 20 akkers, or four shillings, and by nine o'clock in the evening they closed because the girls were tired out.

We returned by train to Mersa Matruh. As always at the junctions of Tanta and Damanhur there were English ladies with trays of cobs and sandwiches and mugs of tea. How good they were, particularly when one was coming down from the desert. Almost immediately on return I found myself attached as a signaller to a troop consisting of one 18/25 pounder gun and eight dummy guns, commanded by Captain Garry Birkin. On 7th December we drove westwards into the desert on what we were told was an exercise, but on 9th December it turned into the real thing, Wavell's offensive.

The South Notts also provided a troop of real guns, but our task with the dummies was to provide a diversion on the eastern side of the Italian strongpoint at Maktila, while the real attack went in from the other side. After

I felt deeply impressed by their determination to leave their own country and make their way to Egypt to volunteer to fight as privates.

the 50 mile approach march to within range of the Italian positions, we set out our stall of dummy guns and the real gun was as far as possible hidden. When it fired, thunder flashes were let off alongside the dummies. My job was to lay the telephone cable from the gun to the observation post. I was doing this on the first morning and making my way through a position of Coldstream Guards.

I was fascinated to talk to one of the guardsmen: he was polishing up his brasses, a task he obviously found essential, battle or no battle. Two hundred yards away was obviously the officers' mess, where two mess servants had set out a couple of trestle tables and were trying to spread them with white table cloths. This had drawn the attention of the Italian artillery, and there were regular shell bursts near them. All this seemed too much like a parody of Guards' behaviour, and I would love to know how it ended. However, I had to get on, but I quickly learned one valuable thing, that fortunately Italian artillery ammunition was very inefficient. Their shells dug quite deep holes when exploding, perhaps 18 inches deep, so that most of the splinters went up in the air, and one could be quite close to a shell burst without harm. Our own shells, by contrast, burst on the surface and their splinters whizzed close above the ground surface all round – very lethal.

That night I took my turn on guard. It was pitch black and we had no idea where the enemy might be, except that he could appear from any direction, and there was the distant thump of shells and rattle of machine gun fire. Never since have I kept such an intense watch, but of course nothing happened. Next day I was line-laying up a shallow wadi and saw a single soldier steadily making his way along the other side about 50 yards away. I heard a single shell coming which seemed to burst right beside the man, completely blotting him from view. I was just thinking "poor chap!" when the smoke cleared and he stood up, and walked calmly on uninjured. I thought that if one could survive that, Italian gunfire was nothing to worry about, and it gave me great confidence.

Next morning our real gun fired a few rounds and a white flag was hoisted over the strong point into which the Italians had withdrawn. To a small party of one gun, a platoon of infantry, eight dummies and a sackful of fireworks, more than 5,000 men surrendered, together with their arms, equipment and guns. They were marched off track to the prisoner of war cage in the hands of half a dozen British squaddies. Most of our army swept on but our part was now ended and we made our way back to Matruh. It would be nice to feel that war was always like this – no casualties and plenty of fun.

To a small party of one gun, a platoon of infantry, eight dummies and a sackful of fireworks, more than 5,000 men surrendered, together with their arms, equipment and guns.

Immediately after our return I got my first stripe. The first garment I sewed it on was a captured Italian pullover that I liked, which shows the pleasantly informal nature of desert wear. Christmas was good with unlimited beer and other goodies sent up from Cairo by the colonel's wife. My time in Matruh came to an end for I was detailed for a signals course at Maadi, near Cairo, starting 28th December. Three memories of Matruh stand out: endless hours of digging, magnificent bathing and the absence of home mail for months at a time. Nevertheless, I wrote to my mother practically every week throughout the war, though topics for letters were not easy when one could not say where one was, or anything in detail of what one was doing.

1941 (JANUARY-APRIL)
CHAPTER 4

LETTER TO A WIFE ON THE DEATH OF A DEAR FRIEND

LETTER TO A WIFE ON THE DEATH OF A DEAR FRIEND

I entered 1941 at the Middle East Signal School. Course No.14 was for both officers and NCOs and ran for six weeks, so at the end of it I felt I really knew my job. Maadi was at the end of 12 miles of electric railway running into Cairo City centre, so I was easily able to get into town in the evening or at weekends. The station was a mile or so from camp so, if possible, one got a taxi. Since taxis were scarce the drill was to jump on the running-board of one going in the right direction. On one occasion I even rode the whole way on the luggage grid. A bit tricky going round corners! The course contained Australians and New Zealanders, which added to the social side. By the time it had ended, the South Notts had left Matruh and handed in their guns.

It must have been at this time the Army apparently thought my regiment was up the desert because I was put on a very small ship in Alexandria which slowly chugged its way up the 800 miles of coast to Tobruk. There I tasted, for the first time, the terribly salty Tobruk water and thought the cooks had made a mistake and used sea water for the tea. After a day or two in a transit camp, my proper destination was discovered and I joined the same ship to chug all the way back again, this time with the holds full of hundreds of Italian prisoners. I finally found my way to the regiment.

I rejoined the unit in February on the Suez Canal. Every night the Germans flew along it dropping magnetic acoustic mines, and our job was to shoot any mine dropped. We were split into posts of four men, each under an NCO and about 500 yards apart. When a bomber flew over on a moonless night it was terribly difficult to see if it had dropped anything, and I don't recall having anything dropped on my particular patch. Our neighbours did, however, and reported it, so a Wellington equipped with a circular electromagnet beneath it flew up and down a number of times without exploding anything. The man who had seen the mine dropped was told he must have imagined it but, sure enough, the next ship to pass through blew up on it. These Wellington minesweepers

1941, Suez Canal, Ted Coup

1941, Suez Canal

were not very effective, and although ships were getting through the canal many were sunk by mines.

Suez, which was within reach, was a non-event, and the best relaxation was swimming. Only strong swimmers could swim right across the canal and back again. One night I was on watch when I was startled to see a huge shape loom out of the darkness above me. It was a patrol of the Egyptian Camel Corps, and they moved so silently that I had never heard them. We fraternized.

After a few weeks of this we moved to Tahag to train for a seaborne landing. Tahag was an enormous permanent camp which seemed to extend for miles. It had six outdoor cinemas, of which three were within walking distance and changed their programmes twice weekly, so that I could, and did, see a different film every night of the week. There were Egyptians serving bottles of beer during the show, and when the audience disapproved they threw empty bottles at the screen. The shouts of "get up them stairs" still echo in my ears.

It must have been around now I became a full bombardier, so pay was a bit better. Camp cinemas all over the Middle East were all owned by Shafto, an Aussie soldier who had stayed on in Egypt after the First World

LETTER TO A WIFE ON THE DEATH OF A DEAR FRIEND

War and had become a millionaire. Alternatively, one could go along to the NAAFI for a choice of egg and chips, sausage and chips etc., and play housey-housey, as bingo was then called.

On 3rd April orders suddenly came to return to the Western Desert. We had already been equipped with 25 pounders but now stores poured in. Other units were ordered to give the South Notts anything they wanted. News of Rommel's attack 1,500 miles away had become common knowledge and on 5th April we set off westwards. We bivouacked the first night at Mena Camp, a few miles north of Cairo. Pete Birkin the battery commander came round and let it be known that the military police in Cairo had been requested to be kind, on this our last night before going up to meet Rommel, and trucks were laid on to take us all into town.

As we approached Tobruk we could hear bombing and shelling from 20 miles away, and at last we crossed the perimeter fence long after midnight. Soon after, barbed wire was drawn across the road and the last belt of mines was laid.

We spent the evening at the Casino Badia, a remarkably good place, frequented by many better class Egyptians. There was an Egyptian band and some very good oriental dancers, prime among whom was Madame Badia's 17-year-old daughter, a beautiful girl. Her mother watched her like a hawk and no-one could get near her. I was intrigued by one of the stringed instruments in the band, which the player assured me was a zarramuta, and I solemnly told him I had never heard a zarramuta better played. We all had quite a party, and I was finally escorted off the stage by an MP. It was Saturday night.

On Sunday morning we set off westwards up the potholed coast road, and on Tuesday reached Sidi Barrani. It had almost 50 mud huts, and here was where Mussolini had earlier reported the trains were running again. As the convoy was passing Buq Buq, despatch riders rode down the column showing boards on which were chalked the words "close right up" and "drive as fast as possible". It appeared orders had just been received to get to Tobruk as quickly as possible, and we were told: "There have been German tanks between here and Tobruk this morning." We were the only vehicles going west, streams of traffic were travelling in the other direction. We wound up the escarpment to Fort Capuzzo and the wire.

On the top was the last petrol point, but no time was wasted, and two cans were thrown into the back of each truck as it passed. We soon used one of ours. It was getting dark as we crossed the frontier into Libya. I was driving, and thinking about enemy tanks, when the engine began to splutter, cough and then stopped. Nothing would induce it to start again. The vehicles behind me all passed, and soon two of us were left alone in the silence and darkness. I knew that somewhere, coming along behind to deal with any broken-down vehicles was the Light Aid Detachment wagon with the sergeant fitter. At last he came, could not find the trouble, and took us in tow.

It was a terribly difficult journey being towed in pitch darkness, and I had to keep on glancing to the side to relieve the strain on my eyes. As we approached Tobruk we could hear bombing and shelling from 20 miles away, and at last we crossed the perimeter fence long after midnight. Soon after, barbed wire was drawn across the road and the last belt of mines was laid. We still did not pull up until the column met a crowd of vehicles and guns coming from the opposite direction. Three regiments met at a crossroads and stayed there until morning.

Morning dawned with a blinding sandstorm and there was immediately an alarm that we were about to be attacked by tanks. The wagon line officer, Lieutenant Newman, obviously inspired by exploits in the Spanish Civil War, passed down the line of vehicles saying in his rather squeaky country voice: "When the tanks come, stick the crowbars in their tracks…" The prospect of approaching a tank in the open desert at close quarters armed only with a crowbar seemed to appeal to nobody, and I did not notice anyone getting crowbars out. Fortunately at midday the flap was over and our guns went into position two or three miles south of the crossroads.

The defended area at Tobruk was larger than people imagine. The perimeter wire ran in a half-circle for about 30 miles from coast to coast, with the town and harbour in the centre, on the shore, of course. Outside the wire was an old anti-tank ditch, and inside was a concrete defensive post with underground shelters every half mile or so. These posts were numbered from the west. Because there was virtually no variation in height near the wire there were several steel

When the tanks come, stick the crowbars in their tracks…" The prospect of approaching a tank in the open desert at close quarters armed only with a crowbar seemed to appeal to nobody

observation posts and towers. The posts comprised a small crow's nest at a height of about 15 feet: the towers were much larger and higher, perhaps 50 feet, with the ladder concealed behind a roll of scrim (open fabric). Some observing officers used them, some found somewhere on the ground, but they looked, and were, terribly vulnerable. Glad to say, I never sat on top of one, like a coconut on a shy.

We were one of four Royal Horse Artillery regiments – two regular, two yeomanry, and a field regiment. The infantry were the 9th Australian Division, and there were a few odds and ends.

It was now Good Friday, 10th April, and shelling had been exchanged for 24 hours. At 3pm an attack came in on our left from enemy tanks which broke through the wire, but at dusk they withdrew after eight had been knocked out by fire from the whole regiment. It must have been about then I was manning an observation post in a shallow slit trench near point 29 with Lieutenant Timms. It was an exciting exercise trying to direct fire on to enemy vehicles and guns, but terribly difficult through the mirage seen through binoculars, and blowing sand. It was Timms' first time at an observation post (mine too, but he didn't know that) so most of the orders were given by Bombardier Middleton.

Next day some enemy infantry had obviously got into the anti-tank ditch and if I popped my head up for air a rifle shot would be fired with the bullet zinging close by. If I had to get out of the trench and go back to our vehicle down by the hill it was a matter of running the gauntlet. The Northumberland Fusiliers, machine gunners, were also behind the hill and we got them to silence the enemy riflemen. They were firing over our heads (like artillery) but the trajectory was terribly close to us and some shots hit the ground very near us and ricocheted on, so we had to stop them. We spent 48 hours at this observation point, which meant I went for three nights without sleep, and when we were relieved I was so tired while waiting for the truck that I lay down on the ground and went straight to sleep.

Back at the gun position I could sleep properly for a short time. Regarding the breakdown of my truck on the night trek into Tobruk, I learned that the mechanic had found paraffin in the engine. The can we had filled up with must have contained paraffin!

It was now Easter Sunday. On the gun position, the information coming down from Lieutenant Bennet at his observation point was relayed to us. Our telephone lines had been cut but the infantry line was still working and orders came to our troop through the two headquarters. He was with the Aussie infantry in point 32 when the German infantry broke through the wire and German tanks

The enemy quickly got the exact range, then plastered us continually for 20 minutes. I suppose between one and two hundred rounds were fired, then they stopped, obviously thinking we were knocked out.

were all around him in his Bren carrier. He described the Jerries using flame throwers, and they were so close that he gave the order "Target ME – fire!". The gun position officer's assistants feverishly worked out his exact position and the guns fired.

The Aussies stayed in their trenches, the observation post party kept their heads down in the corner, and the German infantry were cut up and chased from the gap in the wire. The enemy tanks went on. While all this was happening, a terrific air battle was in progress with 15 Germans brought down for the loss of three of our Hurricanes. The sight of a plane diving vertically to earth became commonplace Easter Sunday! Artillery duels continued.

I accompanied an officer to an observation post in front of a small mound near the wire where we were completely overlooked by the enemy. We did a bit of shooting and then enemy shells bracketed our observation post. We were in a slit trench about three feet deep, two of us, with our driver and the truck in a mere scrape behind the mound. The enemy quickly got the exact range, then plastered us continually for 20 minutes. I suppose between one and two hundred rounds were fired, then they stopped, obviously thinking we were knocked out.

In front, at one point, a spent splinter had hit me on the cheek, but barely drew blood, and one or two shells had landed on the very edge of the trench. I must admit I felt our survival was miraculous. When we were certain the shelling had stopped we nipped round the back of the mound expecting to find our driver dead. But no, despite his only being in a scrape he was right as rain. However, our observation post was obviously untenable, so we got in our truck and moved.

As April went on Stukas were active daily over the town and harbour, which we were able to watch with equanimity from a few miles away. Then one day they suddenly turned their attention to the gun line of 425 Battery. I was up at the observation post, saw the raid from a distance, and returned to hear with foreboding that three senior NCOs had been killed. One was BSM Smedley, a sergeant major of only 21, and yes, one was Phil Collihole. I collected his steel helmet, which had a jagged splinter hole in the back.

We had been very close since the war started, and up to a fortnight before when the battle began we had been able to exchange a few flippant remarks every day. His death left a big gap, and I wrote to his wife as soon as I could. However, there was no time for this now: I was promptly promoted to lance-sergeant and put in his place in charge of battery signals. After this raid Lord Haw Haw announced over the German radio that "all guns in the Palestine area of Tobruk have been knocked out," but in fact Battery 425 was very much in action. My 23rd birthday passed unnoticed.

When the battle had started 11 Hurricane fighters had been left for the defence of Tobruk fortress. Every day we saw one or more shot down, and every day fewer and fewer were able to scramble. Towards the end of April just one was left, and I saw him plummet from 10,000 feet to crash into the ground a few hundred yards away. He was Flying Officer Lamb, a Canadian. Earlier I saw a German plane hit and the pilot descending by parachute. We watched him land and said: "Let's go and do him in." We grabbed rifles and actually jumped into a truck. But after a few minutes sanity prevailed, and we left him for someone else to pick up.

> **I returned to hear with foreboding that three senior NCOs had been killed. One was BSM Smedley, a sergeant major of only 21, and yes, one was Phil Collihole. I collected his steel helmet, which had a jagged splinter hole in the back.**

LETTER TO A WIFE ON THE DEATH OF A DEAR FRIEND

1941 (SUMMER)
CHAPTER 5

COMMANDERS DOWN
...BREAKOUT EXACTS ITS PRICE

COMMANDERS DOWN ...BREAKOUT EXACTS ITS PRICE

On 30th April the Germans made another attack, broke through the wire and captured several posts, thereby establishing a salient within the perimeter, which they retained throughout the siege. Our counter attack was unsuccessful. So ended three weeks of battle, a very wearing experience. The Germans retained their salient but got no further, and things quietened for some weeks, except for nightly bombing.

At this stage somebody decided that I was the only man in B troop who could find his way at night, by driving in darkness (without lights of course) across the virtually featureless desert up to the Aussie position on the salient. I managed this okay, though why I had to go I cannot recall. Next night I had to go again, this time on my own responsibility, to find and mend an observation post's broken telephone line. The post was in the Aussie trenches, only 50 yards from the enemy, and it was not possible to stir by day. Because of the rocky ground the trenches were only two and a half feet deep, so it was a pretty unattractive spot.

I decided the cable break must be in front of the trench, so I wriggled out onto the sand in front, found the break and was about to repair it when a Jerry machine gun opened up. The bullets went zinging past me and I was convinced I had been spotted. I froze and tried to melt into the ground, but the fire seemed to go on interminably. In fact the gun was probably firing on fixed lines. I finished the repair very quickly: it was not an experience I enjoyed.

Next night I had to do this journey a third time, and this time I made a hash of it when nearly there by running one wheel into a slit trench and getting stuck. By the time we got back I was dead beat and actually fell asleep on the gun position while they were firing a barrage. On one occasion I was lying in my blankets in the same shallow slit trench at night while German bombers were overhead, and I heard a bomb coming down. It got louder and louder until I thought it was certain to hit me. Indeed, when it exploded, the edge of the crater was just six feet from the end of the trench where my feet were, and the spent splinters had rattled down all over my blankets. I paced the distance out. I was fortunate that the bomb was a small one, only 50 kilograms.

Two or three of Phil Collihole's friends used the quieter period to go to the military cemetery, where they made a concrete surround and set up a cross over his grave. It took several visits.

In June there was a relief attempt from the frontier. It failed. This was disappointing. About this time a third troop was formed with old 1914 howitzers taken from the 51st Field. It was christened Glamour Troop, after Ian Sinclair commanding it. I laid a phone line to it which was always thereafter called the Glamour Line. Since I extended it to A&B

> **I wriggled out onto the sand in front, found the break and was about to repair it when a Jerry machine gun opened up. The bullets went zinging past me and I was convinced I had been spotted.**

1941, Tobruk cemetry

troop observation posts, it duplicated the posts' ordinary lines, forming a belt and braces job. It was thus very useful when the cry came from a battery telephone exchange "a troop's line's gone!" If I felt it was a difficult assignment I would go myself, taking another man with me.

Usually it involved walking up the line, plugging in with a field telephone at intervals to make sure we hadn't missed the break. Often it had broken because of shellfire: sometimes because a tank had crossed it. Sometimes it ran across a minefield but, fortunately, this didn't matter very much because many were old enemy anti-tank mines and, in any case, the sand usually looked slightly different where the mines had been sunk (though not visible at night).

It was now July, height of the desert summer. Regular bathing parties were laid on - just as well, since it gave the chance to get clean every two weeks or so, and to wash one's clothes. We were issued with seawater soap, which was singularly inefficient, and the only hope of reducing the amount of grime was to beat one's wet clothes on the rocks. And grime there was, after wearing a shirt for a week in a temperature of 100° and in sandstorms.

The water ration was half a gallon per man per day. This provided a pint mug of tea at breakfast, dinner and tea which used three pints: the cookhouse kept half a pint per man for cooking and washing utensils: and each man had one pint for his water bottle every other day. There was thus nothing for washing, either oneself or one's clothes. The water too was salty, nearly as salty as seawater, so the tea was nothing like you have ever tasted.

One of the great pleasures of going on a bathing party was that near this beach was an old Arab well containing absolutely fresh water. The well was not controlled in any way by the Army so on the limited occasions we visited it I would drink my fill, and fill my water bottle. Otherwise I was thirsty most of the time: I think I felt it more than most people. I swore to myself that if I ever got out of this I should revel in drinking water for the rest of my life. I have kept my promise.

Food was monotonous to a degree. Sometimes there was no bread, and we had biscuits. Usually there was bread, but because the flour was thick with weevils the bread had lots of little black bits in – dried weevils. Not that it mattered – one couldn't taste them. The other staple was bully beef, sometimes MV (meat and vegetable in theory but actually pretty disgusting). So the menu every day was like this, for over eight months:

Breakfast: Biscuit porridge, tinned bacon boiled in the tin, which made it soggy and greasy.
Dinner: Bully stew or MV.
Tea: Pilchards or jam.
A pint of tea with each meal.

Just occasionally there was a tin of fruit. I remember to this day that a tin of pineapple was the ration for eight men, and contained 44 pieces. I carefully dished it out at five and a half per man. And I have never eaten a pilchard since! Nevertheless, to get a meal under one's belt was a great thing: one was then ready for whatever might befall, and I retained this feeling for many years.

I also used to control the cigarette ration of 50 a week. To help make them last, two or three men would give me their ration to keep, and would ask for cigarettes as they wanted them. They knew I only smoked 30 to 40 a week and they ran no risk of me being tempted by theirs.

I was thirsty most of the time: I think I felt it more than most people. I swore to myself that if I ever got out of this I should revel in drinking water for the rest of my life. I have kept my promise.

Because of the bombing, ships with supplies could only enter the harbour during the moonless period. Even then there were heavy raids on the port. This also applied to the NAAFI ship which came in once a month, so one probably had a can of beer and a couple of bars of chocolate at that time. Sometimes there would be no mail for two months at a time, then it would all come together but for me usually monthly always from mother and father, occasionally one from brother Peter somewhere in the world.

By August we were rationed to 10 rounds per gun per day, which only provided for a few minutes' firing at dawn and dusk, and although during the period of the siege the Germans would think up some attack every few weeks, there were long periods of quietness. During one such period, since leave was impossible, a rest camp was established where I spent three days. We would take a truck and go for a swim in the afternoon, but apart from that there was nothing to do, and I lay all day on my bed (ie my blankets on the ground). The inactivity made me feel ill, and I was glad to get back to work.

However, we did entertain ourselves. Battery HQ was in a large cave, where we had periodical concerts. We had what would later be called a skiffle group, who included Driver Walker slapping a homemade double bass made out of a packing case and wire (when I next saw him 25 years after the war it was as chairman of a public company!) Many people used to sing, but particularly enthusiastic were the cries for a particular gunner to sing Mexicali Rose, which he did in a falsetto voice.

Various memories come flooding back. Gunner Siddall, the battery storeman, who firmly believed the earth was flat, and obstinately refused to be convinced otherwise. Then there was the habit of catching a scorpion, surrounding it in a ring of petrol which was then lit, and we would watch it sting itself to death. Rarely a chameleon would be found; I put one on a piece of green canvas and waited for it to change colour, but it never did.

Whenever attacking enemy planes came near, which they often did, everyone would blaze at them with rifles. We never did any known damage but it made us feel a lot better. I often read in later years about young men saying: "I would never kill anyone". If they had much experience of a lot of people trying to kill them, they might feel differently. During a war one develops a hard skin, which never quite softens.

There was always some character in any unit who reckoned he could cut hair, so for a few piastres one could maintain a reasonable appearance.

Another form of entertaining ourselves was by throwing Italian hand grenades, which were like little red cylinders. There were thousands of them in the old Italian ammunition dumps and I used to enjoy throwing them at a target trench. Just a bit of fun with a firework, but in due course someone was injured so the practice was forbidden. We had to use explosives too to make a new dugout. I always refer to them as dugouts, although actually one could only get down about two feet and most of the walls were sandbags above ground. Even those two feet took a lot of work with a pickaxe and blasting with gelignite. One would swing a pick and make a hole in the rock, into which a sausage shaped stick of "jelly" was stuck, with short length of fuse. Fuse lit, we ran for 30 or 40 yards. Then came the explosion, and the shower of bits of rock and sand.

Theoretically there were dug latrines, but many of us preferred to go for a short walk with a shovel. One day at the gun position Peter Birkin, the major, was watching through his field glasses and saw Aggie Carr, his observation post officer, a mile forward, squatting down having just taken the traditional walk with a shovel. Enemy artillery opened up all around him and Peter's reaction was to laugh his head off – an example of one's black sense of humour at the time.

Books were scarce and passed around. John Walker had got Gone with the Wind which was much in demand, and of course each man in turn who got it took a long time to read it, but it came to me eventually and I enjoyed it enormously. We were equipped with No.9 wireless sets, which had no speaker. Towards 9pm every night a few men would drift over to my truck to hear the news, and I can hear now the sound of Big Ben in the desert darkness, and see the little cluster of men round the tailboard listening to the single pair of headphones with the volume turned up. Presumably the news was on the Forces service from Cairo, but we were able to hear nothing else because we had to switch off to save the batteries. Keeping all the accumulators charged was a constant preoccupation. They were old; there was no hope of replacements in the siege; and I had to keep the wireless sets constantly ready for action. I can hear the chug now of their little charging engine, running day and night.

The band's instruments had been left a thousand miles away, but Dennis Pike, one of the bandsmen, still had his posthorn. Occasionally he could be prevailed upon to give us the Posthorn Gallop, which was unbearably evocative as it echoed over the desert.

The battery telephone exchange was in a dugout and was an old-fashioned plug-in 10 point thing, but at least reliable. Its primary function was to connect battery HQ and the gun positions to the observation posts. It was, of course, manned 24 hours a day throughout the siege. I used to take a two hour shift every night, indeed I never had an unbroken night's sleep for nine months. But I learned to think of sleep as an active pleasure, not just something one did between 11pm and 7am.

Some time about September I started to feel terribly tired and developed diarrhoea (more than the usual) and it was all I could do to drag myself away from my bed across to meals. Even then I could hardly eat anything, but wanted the tea. This lasted a fortnight and in fact I was beginning to feel a bit better when I went to Harry Day, the medical orderly. He took one look at my eyes and said: "You've got jaundice". By then it wasn't worthwhile going to the medical officer, and I fairly quickly recovered.

Some time in autumn, surprisingly, we began to receive a daily rum ration. Geoff Douglas, a battery clerk, decided very sensibly that while one tot of rum was not much good to anyone, if we saved it up for one week we could have a party. We rewardingly formed the Saturday Club, whereby each Saturday evening four or five of us played auction bridge, which we had just learned, and drank rum. This went very satisfactorily for two or three weeks, and a Saturday then came when we had saved a lot of rum. At the end of this evening we came out of the sand bagged dugout half cut to find Major Peter Birkin outside, absolutely furious. As I told him, I had made proper provision for the manning of the telephone exchange, there was no barrage planned, and so on, but he was unappeased. Next morning we lined up before him, and he said fiercely that unfortunately we were his senior NCOs and he could not possibly do without us in action, otherwise we should have been up before the colonel. So I was unexpectedly saved.

I was up before the colonel only a few weeks later, though, to be interviewed for Officer Cadet Training Unit. The colonel was Bill Seely and the interview went OK, since I was told he would recommend me but that I should have to wait until we got out of Tobruk.

At the end of August most of the Australians were relieved, and replaced by Poles and some British infantry: we were supporting the Polish Brigade. They were charming and brave people - as effective in their frequent night patrols outside the wire as the Aussies had been.

They were much taken aback by the water situation: in the first place they used a week's supply in three days and had to be given extra, which annoyed me intensely. Secondly, they could hardly credit the taste: some tried to improve it with jam, but without success.

Actually, although we did not know it at the time, only five units saw the siege through from end to end. The South Notts was one. An Aussie infantry battalion was another: they were due for relief in October but could not get out before the full moon came round again.

There was always bombing of course, chiefly of the port but also on the gun positions and elsewhere. It was usually at night, during the fortnight of the moon, but also by daylight, since we had no fighters whatever, and anti-aircraft fire did not achieve much. I was once caught out in a daytime raid when I realised that a squadron of enemy bombers was heading direct for me with all machine guns blazing. They were terribly near and low and I had to decide in an instant whether to lie down or run 50 yards to the nearest dugout. I ran, seeing the line of bullets kicking up the sand and approaching at a tremendous rate. I made it with a second to spare.

I realised that a squadron of enemy bombers was heading direct for me with all machine guns blazing.

One night the old Italian ammunition dump was hit. It was little loss to us though we did use a few old Italian guns as what we called Bush Troop, and the ammo went on burning and exploding for hour after hour, providing the most spectacular firework I have seen, for 24 hours.

By this time we had picked up a great deal of old Indian Army language, chiefly Urdu, to which we had added many Arabic words, so the 8th Army's conversation was quite distinctive.

November was bitterly cold and we had changed back into battle dress. We knew the breakout would soon come and all NCOs had the plan of attack explained. We were to break out and join up with the rest of the 8th Army coming up from the Egyptian frontier. My job was to ensure the communications from Ops to guns, this time chiefly by wireless. On the 20th the code word was given, and at 6am next morning the Black Watch were lined up on the start line in the anti-tank ditch. My information came from Bombardier Keeton, who was in charge of the linelaying 15 cwt truck. It was completely unarmoured, although heavily sandbagged, but travelled with the first wave of tanks, immediately behind the infantry, laying out the line as it went.

I ran, seeing the line of bullets kicking up the sand and approaching at a tremendous rate. I made it with a second to spare.

Stan Keeton told me that the Black Watch had a heavy rum ration, so that one or two were left behind at the start. Otherwise the men marched steadily on, led by a piper. When a man dropped wounded or killed he was left by his mates but marked by his rifle stuck in the ground by its bayonet, for stretcher bearers following behind. Stan was perched on the back of this truck reeling out cable, so conspicuous in the middle of an infantry attack that I thought he could not survive. But he did and was awarded the Military Medal for it.

What's more, the line survived too, and by 10.30 was in use to strong point Tiger, which had been the objective. This was later than it should have been: tanks got stuck on an intervening minefield, most of the infantry's company commanders were killed; and there was a thick dust storm everywhere, made even worse by the tanks, so that the leading infantry lost their way – in short, amid the fog of war.

The battle went on until 30th November, with heavy shelling of the gun positions. I had a lot of trouble keeping wireless communications going, and I had to go out to the captured German strong points where our observation posts and infantry were, amongst other things to take fresh batteries.

1941 (NOVEMBER-DECEMBER)
CHAPTER 6

FORAY FOR FAROUK
OUR GUNS TRAIN ON HIS PALACE

Ken Tew was wounded at Bashful operation post by a shell splinter and never returned to the regiment, I believe, though, he was OK after the war. I remember that on the way out there from the wire I used to have to pass a dead Scottish soldier who was stuck in barbed wire with a live grenade in his hand and the pin out. I think the burial parties must have been nervous about touching him. He was kneeling as if poised to throw the grenade.

During a battle one gets so filthy, with no time or possibility of a wash for days. There was usually a sandstorm blowing, which left a layer of dirt on the inevitable sweat, and in particular one had no time (and probably no water) to shave. I remember looking appalling after four days without a wash or shave, I marvelled at how comparatively clean the fair-skinned Bob Foulds looked. He was the number 1 (sergeant) for a gun team.

I usually tried to shave every couple of days, lack of water and blades inhibiting more, but our officers never bothered us. In spite of everything, unlike the First World War, nobody to my knowledge ever got any lice, although fleas were a terrible nuisance. They were not due to us, but lived in the sand everywhere that Arabs had been, and for a long time in Tobruk I slept every night on top of a sandbagged dugout rather than inside, just to avoid the fleas.

Splinters from our own anti-aircraft used to patter down like rain all around every night, but never did me any harm. Incidentally I became expert in catching fleas in the seams of my shirt or trousers and killing them; you crack them between your fingers.

1941, Tmini, Christmas, DGM, Dick Hockin, P. Diath, Dick Richards, Roger Coutin, John Driver, Bob Foulds, Dew John

In winter it was bitterly cold at night, even though still hot by day, and temperature change was enormous. We had by now changed back to battle dress.

The battle went on for about three weeks in all, and eventually we linked up with the New Zealanders. I have always blamed them for looting my dugout while I was away – they took my camera. By 10th December the Germans and Italians were in full flight. At one point I went forward in my 15 cwt to the infantry battalion HQ, an old Italian fort half ruined by shellfire. The building was still being intermittently shelled and the infantry were rather touchy about any vehicle movement, because it drew more shellfire.

Two miles up the road were the Germans and our forward patrol in a Bren-carrier had brewed up, either on a mine or by being shot up. The two crew lay on stretchers in the courtyard at battalion HQ, both burnt nearly black, but otherwise apparently untouched. Their legs feebly crossed and uncrossed. No-one was doing anything for them; there was nothing that could be done. "They'll die, of course," said the medical orderly casually, and indeed they had 100 per cent burns, but the picture always remained in my memory.

We chased the enemy as far as Tmimi, some 80 miles, where petrol ran out. We settled down to spend Christmas in a cold, rainy, bare stretch of desert with no tents and no sandbags to build any dugouts. Major Birkin and a party set off to try to shoot gazelle for Christmas dinner, but found none and returned with three sheep instead, forcibly purchased from a poor old Bedouin in exchange for tea. They were terribly tough – more like goat, and each man had only a tiny portion. Fortunately we had found a store of rotgut Italian wine.

After seven days at Tmimi the regiment moved back to Tobruk, and in early January we were ordered to hand over all our guns and stores to another unit. In fact we put the lot of our signal stores in one great pile; the good with the bad, and left them in the open desert. It worried me to see stuff we had looked after so long being abandoned in this way, but I don't suppose most of it would have been much use.

We then piled into the back of 3 tonners for the long journey back to railhead. We set off along the Trigh Capuzzo, a bumpy, sandy track across open desert, so could only travel slowly. We had to divert south at the frontier to avoid fighting still ongoing, and spent the

> **The two crew lay on stretchers in the courtyard at battalion HQ, both burnt nearly black, but otherwise apparently untouched. Their legs feebly crossed and uncrossed. No-one was doing anything for them; there was nothing that could be done. "They'll die, of course," said the medical orderly casually.**

night in the truck. It was January, I had only a single blanket and was perished so that sleep was impossible. However, we were heading for the Delta so no-one worried, and next day we embarked on the train of cattle trucks, ultimately reaching Tahog Camp in the desert east of the Nile.

At least we had unlimited water, showers, good food, NAAFI's cinemas, all luxuries beyond price. However, I was not there long before I reported to Cairo Officer Cadet

Above: 1941, OCTU, Bob Foulds

Training Unit, which was to occupy the next five months. I imagine I must have had a week's leave in Cairo first, but I have no recollection of it, although it was probably then that I used to go in the afternoon to the roller-skating rink at Bat-el Louk.

There were three of us from the South Notts: Bob Foulds, George Pearson and myself, all sergeants. Bob and I were in the same barrack room and stuck together. We were at Kasr-el-Nil, the old Turkish barracks in the centre of Cairo, with a great parade ground in the middle consisting of two squares. The first night we put on the white band round the cap and prepared for first parade at 6am next morning. There was no reveille, and it was our duty to wake ourselves up, which we did soon after 5am because the barrack room had to be made spotless before parade. The only incongruous note was that each iron bed had its legs standing in cigarette tins of paraffin. This was to prevent the bugs already infesting the place from getting into one's bed. This method was, in fact, totally effective and we were told that all efforts to drive out the bed bugs had failed: it was an old Turkish barracks. We soon learned, however, that the main objective of the two months' basic training at Kasr-el-Nil was to try to break our spirit, which of course

Below: 1941, OCTU, George Pearson

we doggedly resisted.

For instance, after about a week, the inspecting officer came into our barrack room and declared: "It's filthy, disgusting!" It wasn't of course; it was spotless. But we had to get down on hands and knees and scrub the floor again. The regimental sergeant major and two drill sergeants were from the Guards, and we had to march at Guardsmen's recruit pace, 120 paces to the minute compared with the usual 90. To swing your arms at this pace seemed almost impossible, but we learned to do it, and I almost began to enjoy square-bashing, with the RSM giving his orders from a hundred yards away, and Drill-sergeant Tizzick twirling his pace-stick as we marched. Every now and then the RSM would rush up to some unfortunate individual that his eagle eye had spotted from a distance to screech something such as: "That was an idle turn, sir!"

The first month was the danger period for relegation. At the end of the first fortnight we realised that several familiar faces were no longer there. After another week a few more were missing, and so on. They were RTU – returned to unit. We three from the South Notts survived however.

The programme involved lectures every evening from about 5.30 until 7pm, which were supposed to be of general interest and delivered by someone of some eminence, civilian or military. We became so tired that this was an unequalled opportunity to get some sleep and I personally dozed every evening during this period, a habit which has never left me since during lectures. Twice a week we also went out somewhere in vehicles for night exercises, lasting from 8pm until midnight. The desert is so near Cairo that to find a nearby suitable venue was easy: on one occasion we stormed the pyramids of Nile mud at Memphis and came back covered in black dust. There was a general's inspection every single Saturday morning: there were enough generals in Cairo to ensure we had a different one each time. It was a very time consuming proceeding.

We started off at crack of dawn being inspected by our cadet sergeant, then a sergeant, then the RSM and finally, after waiting for his arrival, by the general. During the latter part we had a full band playing, but fortunately the heat was not great, since this was in February and March. Even so, occasionally someone would faint and crash to the ground. Not a soul moved. When observed by the RSM he would bellow "Take 'im away!" and a couple of minions would double up and drag off the body. Once this happened just as we were about to march off and we all had to march over the recumbent figure.

The general's inspection over, we were free for the weekend, except for a (compulsory) voluntary attendance at morning service at St George's Cathedral next door. Bob and I used to go into town together at weekends, probably for cakes at Groppi's, for which I retain the greatest affection. Their patisserie was like something I have never come across before or since, and the ambience of the garden, with its loggias and little tables, was delightful. It was for officers only, a privilege now permitted to us. Often we would come in the evening, when the dance floor was in full swing, the band playing slow foxtrots and tangos. To get a

This simple answer made a deep impression on me; I have never forgotten it – but he was right. We lived by the law of kill, or be killed.

partner one had to be quick off the mark to beat the next man to it. It was frequented by quite nice local girls, indeed was a highly respectable place.

The drill was that you had to make up your mind as to the girl you were going to ask to dance. The second the music started you had to walk briskly straight to her. It tended to be embarrassing if she then declined, but as a rule she didn't. This is where I learned to dance, and evidently so did Bob, because to this day my wife Vivienne long after said we danced exactly alike. Occasionally I joined a party of local young people, French being our common language, and I even once escorted an Egyptian girl to her home in a taxi, although that is as far as I got.

Groppi's was also the place where I learned to summon a waiter by clapping my

1941, OCTU, Mac & Taffy, sergeant major instructors

hands above my head. The first time I did it, it seemed a terribly ostentatious gesture, but soon one thought nothing of it. It is so simple and effective that I often regretted later, when trying to catch a waiter's eye in England, that it is one of many things that are done better elsewhere.

When in the city we had to carry a swagger cane, and were taught how to salute while walking and carrying this. Believe it or not, the whole procedure took 36 paces - disconcerting to any officer who had all this thrown at him. The officer cadet training unit was multinational with British, Australian, New Zealand and South African individuals there… For the first time I made Aussie and Kiwi friends, but the South Africans kept to themselves. Some Britons were from the Honourable Artillery Company, an artillery regiment largely recruited from the City of London, and full of stockbrokers and the like. One in my platoon was Horgan, who wore a monocle, a remarkable sight when drilling in the ranks.

On one exercise the following problem was put to us by the infantry captain in charge of our intake.

"You are in a tank in an attack and an enemy anti-tank crew beside come out of their pit with their hands up. What do you do?"

"Send them back towards our lines."

"No – as soon as you move on they will nip back to their gun and turn it on you."

"Well, get out of your tank and put a round up the breech and blow it up."

"No time, you must keep moving forward."

"Well, what do you do then?"

"Shoot them."

This simple answer made a deep impression on me; I have never forgotten it – but he was right. We lived by the law of kill, or be killed.

One night about 8 o'clock those of us in barracks were hastily and unexpectedly paraded outside with rifles and marched off through the town. We had little idea of where we were going or what for, but eventually we halted and were drawn up in Abdin Square, before the Abdin Palace. Also there was a troop of 25 pounders brought from Almaza, where the Royal Artillery portion of the OCTU was. A small detachment was taken from our number, including a Scottish command sergeant major with the Military Cross (a very unusual decoration for a warrant officer), and I afterwards heard the tale from him.

These few men went into the palace along with the British Ambassador, Sir Miles Lampton, and searched the place until they found King Farouk. He was invited to look out of the window and see the guns trained on his palace. Sir Miles then made his political demands, which the King had no option but to agree on, as a result of which he did not install a pro-German government. So after standing about for an hour or two outside the palace we all marched home.

Another time we had a sudden call to put on a guard of honour for inspection by the Crown Prince of Saudi Arabia. I remember how absolutely pale and white his face was. Unfortunately we got an unexpected order and made the most fearful hash of opening ranks: I blush to this day when I think of it.

After two months, we moved on to three months of specialised artillery training at Almaza, on the edge of town. Things were now much more relaxed. We were commanded by a Captain Gethryn Hewan, and had two BSMs as instructors in gunnery – Dai Gordon and Mac, as is apparent, one very Welsh and one Scottish. Dai taught us to sing the words of The Screw Gun to the tune of the Eton Boating Song. This was a Kipling ballad about the 13 pounder, the gun that used to be dismantled and carried on mules on the North West frontier, and it had been adopted as their song by the Royal Horse Artillery: it became a great favourite with us too.

1942
CHAPTER 7

MONTY MOVES IN
...AND WE LEAD OUR GUNS A DANCE

The work was serious and of practical value, but it is other activities that are better remembered. Bob and I met an extremely nice Jewish girl called Renee Levy, who was I think only 17, and who developed a considerable crush on Bob, who was a very good looking and typically fair haired Englishman.

Bob kept her at a bit of a distance, but together we saw a lot of her and visited her home, a flat in the working class district of Bab-el-Louk. The family were Sephardic Jews, expelled from Spain some 500 years earlier, but who still spoke Spanish at home, so I was able to talk to her mother and sister. Indeed we went to the wedding when her sister Vicky married a New Zealand soldier. It was held at a Church of England church in Ma'Adi, with a party after at the family flat, where a friend sat down and played Egyptian music on an ordinary piano. It was a privilege to have an entree to the home of an Egyptian.

Renee was the Egyptian Ladies Swimming champion and we went sometimes to a big pool out on the Mena Road, where there was a diving board of spectacular height, quite exciting to watch. On journeys like this we usually travelled by tram, with the inevitable poor hanging on the outside.

Groppi's, as I have said, was a constant pleasure, and many cinemas showed English language films. I went to Gone with the Wind with a South African girl from Motor Transport Corps of the South African First Aid Nursing Yeomanry (FANY). Cinemas only started at 9 in the evening, so with this film it didn't end until 1am - not very satisfactory since she only had leave until 11pm. I can't remember how she dealt with it: by climbing the wall, I think.

There was an English bookshop in town, GM's Bookshop. I bought there a complete Shakespeare, and later a Golden Treasury, which would provide a mine of reading on my return to the desert.

We were now near the end of our course and were given instructions about obtaining our officer's service dress and uniform. I went to an Indian tailor called Ghani from whom I got my service dress and a pair of Bedford cord trousers made of such good material that I was still using them 30 years later. I also required some desert boots and a scarf, and we were issued at Almaza with a camp bed, bedroll, canvas washbasin and suchlike.

Already, by now the 6th June, the South Notts had been overrun at Knightsbridge, and virtually the whole regiment was killed or captured. Official military history says: "This day was both a splendid and a tragic episode in the history of the Royal Artillery, for the gunners fought their guns to the last and died where they stood." It is commemorated in the painting by Terence Cuneo, a print of which later hung in our house.

What a stroke of fortune it was for the three of us that we had left the regiment when we did, although we did not view it that way at the time. We felt depressed at rumours of the disaster which were filtering through, and wondered which of our friends had survived and which were gone. However, with the resilience of youth, depression did not last long, although it was only after the war I found out exactly what had happened.

On 20th June 1942, the OCTU final dinner was held. Next day I was a second lieutenant.

> "This day was both a splendid and a tragic episode in the history of the Royal Artillery, for the gunners fought their guns to the last and died where they stood." It is commemorated in the painting by Terence Cuneo, a print of which later hung in our house.

Four of us promptly set off in a large hired American Hudson car for a week's leave in Alexandria. I drove and kept up a steady 80mph on the desert road. Our party consisted of Bob Foulds, Peter Surfleet, Gillick and myself. We had a pleasant week with plenty of swimming. We were parked on the seafront late one night with two nurses and were amusing ourselves by dancing on the roof of the car. An Egyptian policeman came along to find out what was happening: Peter Surfleet, indignant, picked up the nearest cap to add dignity and it promptly fell over his ears, detracting somewhat from the impression he wished to make. I also recall meeting some rather elegant Alexandrian girls in the best hotel: the telephone number of Luisette Sassoon stayed long in my old address book.

On our return we were only on the outskirts of Alexandria when the differential suddenly failed and we were stranded. We pushed the car to a garage only 100 yards away and left it, returning to Cairo by train. Next day we visited the hirer to report what had happened. He wanted us to pay for the car's recovery, but we finished up obtaining compensation for the rail fare we had to spend instead of being able to travel back by car.

We were now at the Royal Artillery Depot at Abbassia Barracks awaiting posting to a regiment. I was called upon to lecture one afternoon, in an enormous marquee full of newly arrived officers, on what life in the desert was like. However, we did not wait long, and Bob was posted to the South Notts Medium Battery, containing the remnants of the old regiment. I was to go to the 104th (Essex Yeomanry) Royal Horse Artillery, and was issued with my pistol.

I joined the lieutenant quartermaster and a driver for the journey in a 15 cwt truck, together with another officer being posted to them. We two travelled perched high on a load of stores on the back of the truck. I have come across better drivers. Soon, as we were going along the desert road to Alexandria, he misjudged a vehicle coming in the opposite direction. The projecting side of the back or our truck hit it, and first thing I knew I was flying through the air, having been fast asleep on top of the load. I hit the ground with a bump to find the truck, having spun round, was coming directly for me. I rolled aside. The other chap was not so lucky: the truck ran over his arm and broke it so badly that he never came back to the unit.

Somehow we arranged an ambulance for him then proceeded on our journey one short. An hour or so later, the driver again misjudged a vehicle coming in the opposite direction, this time by trying to steer too far from it, so that his near wheels ran into the soft sand on the verge and we shot off and

Battle of Knightsbridge by Terence Cuneo

Terence Cuneo

FORAY FOR FAROUK OUR GUNS TRAIN ON HIS PALACE

*Above left: 1942, OCTU, DGM, Bob Foulds, Bill Williams. Above right: 1942, Cairo, OCTU, Peter Surfleet, Bob Foulds, DGM
Below: 1942, OCTU, Said, Bob, Bill, DGM*

MEMOIRS OF A NOT TOO SERIOUS HUSSAR

Top left: 1942, Alexandria, Bob Foulds, Bob Savours, unknown
Top right: 1942, Alexandria, Bob Foulds, Bill Williams, DGM
Above: 1942, Alexandria

FORAY FOR FAROUK OUR GUNS TRAIN ON HIS PALACE

1942, OCTU

were stuck. We dug ourselves out, put the driver on the back of the truck, and thenceforth I drove.

We spent the night at some transit camp, and only after we had driven for hours next day did I discover I had left my newly issued pistol behind at the camp. This was a serious matter and my heart sank like lead: I was about to join my first regiment under a cloud. I knew it was very difficult to replace a pistol, since pistols were in controlled stores and strictly recorded, but by a merciful chance the officer I was travelling with was the regimental quartermaster and, as we all know, quartermasters are capable of any fiddle.

I had helped him, by taking over the driving of the truck from the driver who was intent on killing us, (the quartermaster was virtually a non-driver) and he, somewhat reluctantly, agreed to replace the missing pistol when we reached the regiment, which he did. So I reported comparatively happily to the regimental HQ of 104th (Essex Yeomanry) RHA to find I was posted to their anti-tank battery. All my training had been with 25 pounders, field guns, and I knew nothing whatever of anti-tank operations, but I was soon to find there was nothing very technical to learn. An eye for country was the main thing.

I was driven over to 237 Battery, one of the four batteries of the 64th Anti-Tank Regiment, and only temporarily attached to the Essex Yeomanry. I never met any of the latter, and we were soon to be regrouped as an anti-tank regiment. In peacetime it had been a territorial battalion of the Royal Welsh Fusiliers, converted to anti-tank at the start of the war, and in spite of now being gunners they were very conscious of their Welshness. The sergeant major, Dai Thomas, always wore the RWF flash sewn to the back of his battledress.

The first man I met was Dick Hockin, a calm, pleasant Yorkshireman who, in civilian life, was in the family woollen business. He took me over to introduce me to Ellis Evans, the battery commander, who was sitting in the back of a 3 ton truck which he had made his home. Dick confided that everybody thought him pretty selfish to do so, since he also had a Jeep; the 3 tonner was supposed to be a stores truck. However, he seemed friendly enough, as did everybody – it was, of course, like first day at a new school. The others were: Roger Courtin, battery captain responsible for administration (dentist in civilian life, with a wife he wanted to be rid of and another woman he wanted to marry).

Dick Richardson, recce officer, also a captain, and an estate agent from Brighton (tall, dark hair, unmarried and with dashing moustache, he would have been at home in the RAF).

The four troop commanders were: Dick Hockin (B Troop, unmarried);

Nick Smith (EW Nicholson-Smith, A Troop, a man of many parts, and a product of Manchester Grammar School. At 27 he had already done nearly five years as a medical student when the war started, but had thrown it up to join up. Previously a labourer, bulldozer driver, commercial artist, married with no children;

Peter D'Eath (slim, fair, good looking. D Troop), a pathological liar who always had to cap anyone else's story. Before the war, one tale went, he had been a professional footballer;

Fourth, finally, was to be myself, in charge of C Troop. How many men? About 25, I think, and four x 6 pounder anti-tank guns,

1942, May, Nottingham Journal

Middle East

MRS. J. M. MIDDLETON, of 64, Burlington-road, Sherwood, sends us the following "Pen Pictures" written by her son who is serving with a famous Notts. regiment in the Middle East, she feeling it may interest other mothers equally with herself.

Pen Picture I.

I will try to give you a couple of pen-pictures; of a church service on Sunday evening, and a concert on Monday. The church service was held in a cave, dimly lighted by the daylight filtering in through a hole in the roof. From the back I can see rows of bodies silhouetted against the light, as the padre rapidly slips his robes over his khaki shirt, and starts. The grand old words of evensong echo through the cave, the Magnificat is chanted, and the hymns are sung with vigour. I love to hear the austere beauty of plain song, all the lovelier for being unaccompanied and in such simple surroundings.

which travelled on portees (open-backed trucks to be released down ramps onto the ground to fire). My Troop Sergeant Porter was an admirable man, immensely competent and pleasant.

The British had only recently stopped retreating, and were at what we were later to know as the Alamein line. My regiment was about 10 miles behind, and I arrived in early August at about the same time that Montgomery arrived to take command of the 8th Army. Almost immediately he prepared a battle plan which he explained in person down to, I think, majors. The battery commander came back and passed it on to us, his junior officers. The attack was expected during the period of the full moon, between 20th and 31st August: the enemy would not risk an attack on our main line, running 30 miles south from the coast, but would come in on our southern flank then turn north to surprise us: in fact, he would come on to exactly where we had an anti-tank screen prepared for him.

The British had only recently stopped retreating, and were at what we were later to know as the Alamein line.

We dug gun positions, but kept our guns out of them, well back, each troop in a separate dispersed little group. Every morning before first light, and again at dusk, we towed our guns into position ready for attack. After it was light in the morning, or dark at night, we towed them back again, and waited. Day after day we had nothing to do but wait, and in the August heat of the desert it was scorching. Plus, I had many skin troubles. The medical officer I went to daily said they would only be cured in hospital. I told him I could not possibly go at a time like this.

1942 (AUGUST)
CHAPTER 8

BOOKS AND BEDOUINS
...AND MENACING MINES

BOOKS AND BEDOUINS ...AND MENACING MINES

We were given the codeword Twelvebore. When a messenger delivered this codeword it would mean the German attack had started and we were immediately to take up our gun position.

Nothing happened for nearly a fortnight. Then in the middle of the night of 31st August Dick Richards the recce officer tore up in his Jeep to say the German attack had started. We rapidly towed our guns into position at Point 106 on top of the Alam Halfa ridge, and waited for daylight. What would later be known as the Battle of Alam Halfa had begun; few battles have a name until afterwards.

Dawn broke on a remarkable sight. Spread out over the plain below me was the whole of the Afrika Korps, at this stage their leading tanks being some miles away. On the far side to the south west rose Himeimat, a sugar-loaf desert hill marking the edge of the Qattara Depression, which was impassable for tanks so the Germans could not outflank us by going deeper into the desert to the south. All day I watched them slowly advance eastward (in Egypt's direction) until we were spotted and came in range of a wretched 88mm. I hated these guns: they had a very high muzzle velocity so the shell would arrive before you heard it and you could not mentally prepare for the explosion: there was no warning. In addition an 88mm shell, like our 25 pounders, did not waste energy by creating a deep crater: it exploded on the surface so that lying flat was not much protection.

A man was wounded, not one of ours: a shell splinter had come out of his behind, tearing away a large piece of his buttock, which we carefully replaced. I took him down to our regimental aid post on a stretcher placed on the back of my 15 cwt. Fortunately no-one had to carry him far. I remember once carrying a wounded man on a stretcher between two of us somewhere back from a forward position for quite a long way, and it seemed a terrible weight.

Back with my guns, I waited to see which way the German tanks would turn, whether north towards us, or east to the tanks of the County of London Yeomanry which were spaced out in a partly hull-down position about a mile from us. They were Grants, the predecessor of the Sherman, and were the first halfway decent tank the British Army had, but still inferior to the German Mark IVs. Our tanks had always been rubbish compared with German, rather like matching an Austin Allegro against a Mercedes in the car world.

A man was wounded, not one of ours: a shell splinter had come out of his behind, tearing away a large piece of his buttock, which we carefully replaced.

I had a grandstand view as one after another our County of London Yeomanry tanks were hit and brewed up. They were all petrol fuelled in those days and caught fire far more easily then diesel powered. I learned after the war that the Germans called them Ronsons!

Watching through my field glasses, I would see smoke and flames suddenly pour

MEMOIRS OF A NOT TOO SERIOUS HUSSAR

Above: 1942, July, Cairo, Peter Surfleet, George Pearson, Bob Foulds, DGM, Bill Williams
Below: 1942, Empire, DGM and unknown

from a tank then the turret would fly open and any unwounded crew would leap out, probably burning. It was a tragic sight, but when the Germans came on many of them were knocked out by anti-tank guns of the Rifle Brigade, and as night came on they retired and went into laager where they were bombed all night by the RAF - laager being the old Boer practice of forming a defensive circle of wagons at night. In mobile desert warfare we used to do this, but later formed more scattered and dispersed groups so that enemy bombing would be less effective. By 2nd or 3rd September dawn broke with the whole Afrika Korps retreating westwards. Without detailing the battle further here, it had gone as Montgomery had forecast to us, and was a great morale booster.

The battle over, I gave way to the MO's suggestion and agreed to go to hospital with all my various skin troubles. I had begun to fall to pieces. I had severe boils, particularly on the neck: desert sores, of course, athlete's foot, a cyst on my chin, and what looked like impetigo was beginning on my face. In spite of my six months in the Delta at OCTU, my previous 18 months in the desert was now taking its toll. So I was taken back, first to the regimental aid post, then to the casualty clearing station and ultimately down to the 6th South African General Hospital in the desert east of the Delta. I found myself in a long ward in a single storey building ministered to by pretty blonde nurses! Our own Queen Alexandra nurses in British hospitals were, by my standards as a young man of 24, old battleaxes.

Next day I had a cyst removed under a general anaesthetic, but I seemed to be kept in bed for days and weeks until all my ailments gradually disappeared. I felt a fraud, particularly being in a surgical ward surrounded by genuine casualties. Next to me was an RAF navigator with a broken neck, incurred in the third accident he had suffered, and remember: he was only a navigator, and the accidents had always been caused by the pilots. A bit farther away was a young infantry officer with a bullet wound in his back. The bullet had gone in below the shoulder and come out again further down – an amazing escape – and they used to pull through the hole every morning.

At last I was away and to the base depot at Almaza in Cairo. By now it must have been mid-October 1942, and knowledge that a big attack was about to take place spread among us. The Battle of Alamein started on the night of 23rd October.

I was desperate to get back to my regiment, because it was the only home I had, though no doubt I was fortunate that things happened the way they did. However, sometime in November I was, thank God, posted back to my unit and ultimately arrived to find them at Tmimi, west of Tobruk. Tmimi was presumably a place on the map, but I never saw so much as an Arab hut, and 237 Battery was spread over an area of desert scattered with camel thorn, and with a low hill, Ras Chicheban, just to the east of us.

Ellis, the battery commander, had waited as long as he could for me to come back from hospital. But ultimately he had to hand the troop over to someone, and Nick Smith got it. By now we had two new officers as reinforcements, Bob Atkinson and John Driver. Bob was young, immature and dull, but harmless: John was an aggressive Labour supporter, and ate his food like a pig in a trough, and was quickly disliked by all.

I was given A Troop with Mahoney as my troop sergeant. He was a trying man, although capable, because if anything upset him (which frequently occurred) he was given to fits of sulking. My driver was Lance-bombardier Jones, a Welshman who had been a miner, and who rather surprised me

I had begun to fall to pieces. I had severe boils, particularly on the neck: desert sores, of course, athlete's foot, a cyst on my chin, and what looked like impetigo was beginning on my face.

by supporting his trade union who were at that time striking back home – war or no war. We were to stay at Tmimi for three months, while the fighting moved further and further ahead of us, since there was only enough petrol and transport for one corps, and we in 10 Corps stayed put. Though we had no idea this would last for long we obviously had to keep the troops occupied, so we resumed training, and also organised a great inter-troop competition. It included many items, of which I remember only a few. Apart from turnout - of men, guns and vehicles - there were contests for manhandling guns and changing a wheel on a Jeep. The way to win

this was to have a strong man hold up the back of the vehicle by sheer brute force as the wheel was removed and the new one put on, and we achieved a very quick time.

The troop that won the competition over all was to be the first and only troop in the battery to have the new 17 pounder guns when they arrived, and they were expected before Christmas. A Troop won and I was delighted to have these new and huge guns with an anti-tank killing range of 2,000 yards, compared with about 800 yards for the 6 pounder.

We trained, of course, and early one morning Ellis Evans took out his officers, about six of us in two vehicles, on some kind of a tactical exercise without troops (TEWT). This was a rare event because we had virtually no petrol. Ellis and two others were leading in his Jeep, and I was in the 15 cwt truck behind. Because there were only two seats in the front I was standing in the back, immediately behind the cab. Suddenly, without warning, there was a tremendous explosion, and the truck stopped. All was silent.

As I recovered from a daze I realised a rear wheel of the truck had set off a mine, and for some reason the front wheel had passed over it harmlessly - just as well for Dick Hockin sitting in front, because had it exploded then it would have taken his leg off. There was a gaping jagged round hole in the steel floor of the truck behind me, so I had been pretty lucky too. We decided it was only because a lot of soft sand covered the mine it was triggered by the second wheel passing over it.

We were now stationary in the middle of

an anti-tank minefield, and Ellis in his Jeep had stopped beyond. We were not particularly worried about walking about, because German Teller mines were not normally set off by the pressure of a foot. First thing to do, though, was to drive on in Ellis's tracks and turn round in what we hoped was safety beyond. Hock took over from the driver. Gingerly he drove back at a snail's pace, keeping his wheels in the tyre tracks, back the way he had come. Ellis walked backwards in front of him directing him, while we all held our breath, hoping a second pressure would not trigger some mine over which we had already passed. But all was well, Ellis brought the Jeep back in the same tracks, and we all drove back to breakfast.

Our mess was a little tent containing a trestle table with room, I suppose, for eight people. It grew dark very early and nights were long, so we had to entertain ourselves. We sang, of course, in particular I remember Widdecombe Fair, with each man allotted to sing one of the names – Peter Gurney, Peter Davey, etc. We designed a house for Roger Courtin, which started off in a modest way but finished up as a large mansion with two wings.

We had all read The Magnet as small boys and reminisced about the characters: it was amazing how much we remembered. Someone would come to breakfast in the morning and triumphantly announce some name he had remembered in the night. I can recall Dick Hockin marching in to breakfast and saying simply: "Dutton, the deaf boy!" I had a little star map with me, and at night I used to go outside and stare at the sky for ten minutes to memorise it then come into the tent and identify what I had seen. To the best of my recollection our light was a hurricane lamp. To see the same stars that I knew at home was comforting.

And we talked: how we did talk! Perhaps it took the place of what a younger generation had at university. In particular I struck up a friendship with Nick Smith, which was to last some years after the war. He was the first (and last) really stimulating man friend I had found since Phil Collihole, and such things are what make war tolerable. He, having been a commercial artist as well as a medical student, was a brilliant cartoonist.

He was completely amoral, but in those days I was very tolerant and accepted people for how I found them. I do not, of course, refer to sexual morality. For instance, when he had been stationed in Gibraltar earlier in the war he decided he was ready to go back to England. So when an Army circular was issued asking for medical students to be trained for the Royal Army Medical Corps he volunteered. Having got back to England, he announced after some time that

I used to go outside and stare at the sky for ten minutes to memorise it then come into the tent and identify what I had seen. To the best of my recollection our light was a hurricane lamp. To see the same stars that I knew at home was comforting.

he had changed his mind and rejoined a fighting unit.

He was fond of riding, and we had long talks about the techniques of horsemanship. He also introduced me to poetry. He travelled everywhere with the Oxford Book of English Verse and the Golden Treasury. He lent me them, but soon I was able to get hold of a Golden Treasury through someone going down to Cairo. I have it still, tattered and soaked though it has been. One thing we were not short of was Canadian Club type whisky, which the mess appeared to receive in an unlimited amount, and our long night talks were well lubricated.

I slept in a little tent of my own, about the size of a bivvy, but with walls about two or three high, so that I could stand up, and get a camp bed in it. Fortunately, although water was limited, of course, there was no rationing as at Tobruk and, what's more, it didn't taste salty.

The gun tiffy (artificer), L/Bdr. Ellis noticed me shaving with a tiny bit of mirror and kindly made me a good wooden-framed one. I used it during the rest of the war and had it long after.

Two or three times Nick Smith and I got hold of a little petrol and went off on a day's expedition in his Jeep. Unfortunately at this time I had no Jeep, which was needed for this kind of thing because it had low reduction gear and 4-wheel drive, which would get out of any difficulty. To be stuck in soft sand was a common problem, although long experience taught one how to avoid it usually. Nevertheless, most trucks carried on their sides sand channels or sand mats to help.

I remember these "swans" very vividly. We once drove across open desert to the west at El Ezzeyat, meeting no one. This was a ruined and deserted Arab village of mud huts, but it must have been visited not long before because, in front of a little mud mosque, was a thing like a bird bath with three or four small coins in the bowl – offerings. Most striking, however, was in the courtyard a single fig tree, apparently the only tree for 50 miles around, and on top a raven's nest. I climbed to it, and inside were two eggs! I suppose this must have been in early February 1943: even in England ravens start laying in February.

A day most clearly in my memory was when we drove south, deep into the desert. We met no-one; certainly no army was to be seen all day. The feeling of solitude was tremendous. We walked all about a shallow, wide wadi. There had obviously been a rare winter rain, because although the ground was now perfectly dry it was covered with a flush of little flowers which would only bloom for a few days. We counted over 30 varieties, and identified many. There were swallows about, probably the selfsame which had been in England two or three months before. Desert wheatears were common, and occasionally a desert rat would pursue its jinking course across the sand.

We struck deeper into the desert, and cresting a low hill, saw in front of us a small encampment of low, black, Bedouin goatskin tents. We stopped, and two men came running out to meet us. One brought with him a tin bowl containing about a quart of sour sheep's milk, full of curds.

We obviously had to drink this to avoid offence, which we did between us, and the other man indicated by signs that he wanted to provide something else, which personally I could have done without. I found and handed over a mess tin and he went off to a camel grazing 100 yards away and proceeded to milk her into it. When he returned I raised the warm camel milk to my mouth with some trepidation, but it was delicious, if slightly salty. We then went into one of the tents and squatted down. The long front was lifted up entirely so we were well exposed to the tribal gathering, and the women were in an open tent a little distance away.

The Libyan Arabs, having been under the heel of the Italians and Germans, were pro-British, and indeed after the war we gave them their independence.

Conversation was, of course, difficult, but we achieved some communications with my few words of Arabic and by signs. The Libyan Arabs, having been under the heel of the Italians and Germans, were pro-British, and indeed after the war we gave them their independence. The old grandfather was suffering from cataracts in both eyes, and wanted to know if we could do anything for him. We told him that he would have to go to Alexandria, which he understood. After half an hour or so we swore friendship and made our farewells.

1942-43
CHAPTER 9

DIRECTION AT LAST
MASTERING THE PANZERS

DIRECTION AT LAST MASTERING THE PANZERS

Before Christmas the colonel insisted on establishing a regimental mess. By name Wyrley Birch, he was a Rhodesian, one of three Rhodesian officers in the regiment who would later become four. On Christmas Eve we were all having dinner when the mess servant came in and announced that there was an old Arab outside the tent door with a camel. After dinner we went out to him in the darkness.

He turned out to be a delightful old boy with a note written by an escaped British officer saying this man had helped him, and asking that someone should try to reward him. He was given some food to take away, but there seemed nothing else we could do, so he was directed rearward to the area of superior headquarters. However, he folded up his camel and settled beside it for the night with a little fire of camel thorn, having given us an admirable demonstration of making his camel rise and fold up again at word of command. In the morning he had gone.

On Christmas morning 1942, in accordance with tradition, we the officers, served Christmas dinner to the men in our battery at midday. There was some beer, not a lot, and they sat at long trestle tables in the open air. Everybody was cheerful: we were not in action, and while most people moaned about being away from Britain, the delivery of mail was pretty good. Food, while extremely monotonous, was reasonable, and somehow the Royal Army Signals Corps had provided some kind of poultry for Christmas dinner. We had our own dinner at night.

Next month I received news of the death of Grandpa, which had occurred on the 17th December. I wrote to my mother every week, and she wrote to me likewise. Because I could say nothing of consequence, and because things changed little, it was not easy. One of my duties was to censor the letters of my men; only one out of 28 was illiterate - better than today's average.

Early in 1943 we received a visit from Duncan Sandys, a very big noise indeed. What he was doing in Egypt at that time I don't know, since he was then Financial Secretary to the War Office. Although I didn't know then, he had been a gunner colonel and, disabled in action, he returned to politics and government: we did know, however, that he was Churchill's son-in-law. My troop had been selected to demonstrate the new 17 pounder gun for him, and I chose No.4 gun team, Sgt. Davies. He was another sulky one, like Mahoney, but the best layer in the troop. A square target was set up 2,000 yards away; Duncan Sandys arrived; Davies laid the gun and fired.

He hit the target smack in the middle and everyone was delighted. Anti-tank guns of course fire only armour-piercing shot. Although shaped like a short shell it is solid, like a cannon ball, and if you are on the receiving end it ricochets a long way along the ground. It would not penetrate a tank on the ricochet but it would and did, carry off a man's leg just like a cannon ball at Waterloo.

Once or twice we had a Sunday morning church service, conducted by the regimental padre. Everybody in the battery was in a big circle, and the short service was always marked with cries to the padre demanding

1942, Christmas, Much love from mother

1942, Christmas day, 237 battery

Bread of Heaven. The hymn is, in fact, Guide Me, O Thou Great Jehovah, to the tune Cwm Rhondda, and it was a tremendous favourite with this Welsh regiment, sung with great vigour and harmony.

Guard mounting usually took place at 6pm, there being six men, two on at a time with two hours on and four hours off, until 6am. Seven men were always detailed for guard, the custom being that the smartest man at the officer's inspection was released from duty. He was indicated by the officer's stick and was known as "stick man" (spoken with equal accentuation on both words). The smartest man of our whole battery was invariably Darkie Taylor, a Liverpudlian of West Indian descent. I never knew him serve a guard – when not in action, of course.

A visit I enjoyed a good deal was that of a small ENSA concert party. There were four of them, two men and two girls, and I take my hat off to them. It was the only ENSA party I saw in the whole war, and for them to come away from the Delta and 500 miles up into the desert, the real desert, was unprecedented. They entertained under the most primitive conditions, and the comedian seemed immensely funny. I wished they'd known how well they were remembered 50 years afterwards.

We must have been at Tmimi until March because we celebrated St David's Day there in the regimental mess. This was, of course, 1st March, and in an old Royal Welch Fusiliers unit a great fuss was made about it. Leeks had been procured – leeks, for heaven's sake, in Egypt – in the desert! A leek was required after dinner particularly for the toast of St David, when a junior officer had to stand on his seat, with one foot on the dinner table, and eat a raw leek, while theoretically a drum was beating. This honour was allocated to John Driver, who was not popular, but had he had the sense to make a good attempt at it his stock would have risen. However, he just about took one bite then pretended to fall down unconscious, which merely made him an object of derision.

Almost immediately after, this halcyon period was at an end, and the whole division moved up some 1,300 miles to an area south west of Tripoli. The journey took some days, over open desert mostly. This usually consisted of clumps of camel thorn a yard or two apart, each clump on a raised hummock of sand. They were impossible to avoid when driving, so the truck banged and bumped its way over humps all day, the springing of these Ford 15 cwts being like iron. On top of this my driver, now an Irishman called Lawson, had the habit of giving a sniff every 30 seconds, and nothing could stop him. To prevent him driving me mad I ultimately had to banish him to the back of the truck and drive myself.

During the long halts I used to sit reading my Complete Shakespeare. One of my sergeants came up and said: "Must be a good book, that, sir." He was disappointed when I told him what it was. I read many Shakespeare plays about this time. Occasionally an Arab would appear from nowhere holding up an egg and saying "Eggies!" in hope of a sale.

On arrival at the assembly area beyond Tripoli, every officer in 10 Corps who was to take part in the attack on the Mareth Line was called to a cinema in Tripoli, which General Montgomery would use to brief us on the coming battle. This was the first time I had seen Monty. He appeared on stage and said: "You have half a minute in which to cough, and thereafter there will be no coughing until I have finished." And there wasn't. He described his plan of the coming battle for two hours, without a note.

It was a tour de force, and we remember how, six months before, the battle of Alam Halfa had taken place just as he had forecast. It was tremendously satisfying to know what was supposed to happen, with a high degree of confidence that this is what would happen. A frontal attack was to go in, but the New Zealand Division and our own 1st Armoured Division were to carry out what he called a left hook, which involved our going deep into the desert southwards, round the end of the Matmata Hill and up northward again on the enemy's flank.

Meanwhile for a few days we faced the Matmata Hills, a few miles away. They consisted of an apparently vertical cliff which we knew contained German machine gun nests. They also had forward troops among the wadis below, and we saw in the battery a communiqué which said the Gurkhas had sent out a fighting patrol the night before and killed 50 Germans: "no prisoners were taken." We were delighted, although we might have thought it did not augur too well for one's own chance of being taken prisoner. The tale went that the Gurkhas used to cut off an ear of anyone they killed and came back with their ears in matchboxes.

On 23rd March we were suddenly ordered to move at 7.30pm and the whole division set off on the 200 mile trek to join the Kiwis. It was not an easy march, and one of my gun towers irretrievably broke down, so the gun had to be brought on behind Mahoney's 15 cwt. He got there all right, but at the cost of his own engine being ruined. I think we then got a spare vehicle of some kind to tow the gun, but Mahoney's truck had to be left. The New Zealanders attacked at 4pm, and at 6pm the order came down from Raymond Briggs the divisional commander: "Speed up, straight through, and no halting."

The division moved forward in about six lines, and at my humble level all I could do was to follow the vehicle in front. It was soon pitch dark, and although the moon was supposed to rise about 11pm, it was cloudy. I couldn't even check that all my guns were behind me, because as soon as one had dropped out I couldn't possibly leave and look for it.

All night we moved forward, often stopping for long periods while the forward

> **On arrival at the assembly area beyond Tripoli, every officer in 10 Corps who was to take part in the attack on the Mareth Line was called to a cinema in Tripoli, which General Montgomery would use to brief us on the coming battle. This was the first time I had seen Monty. He appeared on stage.**

tanks dealt with opposition. We could only see the sky lit by a burning tank or vehicle, usually German: I had no idea where we were, or what was happening – talk about the fog of war! Away on the left flank, although I did not know it, was Bob Arnold, whom I would only meet for the first time years after the war: he was a gunner in a tank of the 9th Lancers.

At dawn we stopped. Most of my guns behind had become separated, but soon arrived. Then the colonel dashed up to say that we were being attacked by German tanks from the right, and took me off in his Jeep to tell me where to place my guns. Since a blinding dust storm was blowing, and the ground was featureless anyway, I found it very difficult to return to the position that Wyrley had indicated.

However, I did my best, riding in the leading gun tower, but the wretched driver drove straight over the body of a wounded German. He could easily have avoided him, but I think he was stricken by panic, and also thought he was dead. It didn't make much difference since the Jerry was shot through the head and unconscious, and obviously would not live anyway. When the flap was over we carried him to the regimental aid post) which the medical officer had established nearby. He was a Nottingham man called Bignal, whose cousins I had been at school with.

There was no sign of the Jerry tanks. We soon learned they had been driven off by one of our batteries, which had destroyed two. The Germans obviously thought that at 2,000 yards they were out of range, and our 17 pounders took them by surprise. They were the 15th Panzer Division, whom we had faced so many times over the years. In the words of the official History of the Second World War they were "quickly repulsed by the 17 pounder anti-tank guns of 76th Anti-Tank Regiment RA." Actually, at some stage since I joined them, what was the 64th Regiment had become the 76th Regiment – why or when, I cannot conceive.

It was now the morning of 27th March, the enemy had retreated and by the 28th the 10 Corps had occupied El Hamma. This was only an Arab village, but the Arabic word hamma means baths, and there were hot springs. David Matthias, Dick Hockin and I went in and found the baths, cut out of natural rock, with steaming hot water flowing through rock-carved cubicles. After a battle and days of no washing, to stand in the hot water and sluice oneself, something that I had not known for six months since Cairo, and the others longer, was marvellous beyond belief.

In the words of the official History of the Second World War they were "quickly repulsed by the 17 pounder anti-tank guns of 76th Anti-Tank Regiment RA." Actually, at some stage since I joined them, what was the 64th Regiment had become the 76th Regiment – why or when, I cannot conceive.

1943 (APRIL-MAY)
CHAPTER 10
TAKEN PRISONER
...AND CUT ADRIFT

TAKEN PRISONER ...AND CUT ADRIFT

We had now been in Tunisia for some days, but it was only as we moved forward that the country began to change. Although still very open, signs of cultivation appeared, occasional trees, wide stone banks, like Pembrokeshire. It was very refreshing after years of desert. We moved on the inland flank of the 8th Army and were not where the action was for some days. Whenever there was a halt, out would come the half petrol tin full of sand from each truck, petrol sloshed on and lit, and in no time an old tin of water would be simmering for a brew.

Every truck carried a blackened brew-can hanging on the rear. Most also had hens, sometimes in the toolbox, sometimes in the case of a gun tower, or on the spare wheel on top, covered by camouflage netting. The hens had been acquired from Arabs in exchange for a tin or two, and at least it meant we could have the occasional fresh egg. It was all most domestic. My truck had a hen which we decided must meet its end, so I decided to wring its neck. Unfortunately this turned out to be more difficult than I had thought. When I had finished I put the dead bird beneath my seat as we drove along. In ten minutes I heard a gentle clucking coming from beneath the seat: the poor bird was still alive! I handed it over to Sergeant Mahoney and how he dealt with it I do not recall.

At Le Kef I was invited into a Frenchman's house for a meal, along with David Ross another officer of the regiment, in a welcome to the liberating troops. It was a super meal, but we failed badly in the singing afterwards, knowing no French songs. As we moved further towards Tunis the 1st and 8th Armies joined up, and we were issued for the first time with rations that came through the 1st Army. These seemed ambrosia. After years living on bully and tinned meat and vegetables we had a compo box for so many men, containing tins of stewed steak, delicious puddings such as creamed rice and treacle pudding.

Various individual pictures remain in my mind from the fighting in Tunisia. In one place, for instance, there were many dead cattle which had been killed in shellfire. They lay with distended bellies and four legs stuck stiffly in the air, giving out an appalling smell. They were far too big to bury, and someone tried burning one by throwing petrol over them, without success. We just had to stick the smell for a day or two until we moved on.

At another place I had the pleasure of seeing three enemy planes being brought down within a few minutes. The last one was an Italian fighter flying low up the wadi in which we were, and which was engaged by a Bofors AA gun near us. The Bofors had an unmistakable sound of "tring-tring-tring" at half second intervals and I must have seen thousands of rounds fired without success, so it was exciting to see a direct hit and the plane plough into the ground a few hundred yards from us. Near us at this time were the Free French forces who had marched across the Sahara from Chad. They included the Goums, in what looked like brown dressing gowns, who had a fearsome reputation for committing atrocities.

On one night march, when the orders were just to follow the vehicle in front, my wretched driver fell asleep at a halt while

I was checking my guns behind, and I came back to find the convoy had disappeared. Here was a pickle! There was no sign of anyone else and the night was black as the inside of a sack. I couldn't go on – I had no idea where to – so I felt there was nothing to be done but wait until morning and hope someone would come back to look for me. This was a bad moment, because I felt I had failed.

Dawn revealed we were alone in an area of knocked-out German tanks. There was a Tiger, the first I had seen, but at least it showed that they could be knocked out. The Tiger, which had only recently appeared, had a fearsome reputation, with thicker armour and a longer range gun than anything we possessed. It could wreak a great deal of damage from a range, which gave it impunity.

Beside this Tiger lay the head of one of the crew. I was worried about anti-personnel mines: these were liable to be anywhere. When trodden on, such a mine sprang into the air like a jack-in-the-box to about waist height, taking your legs off and probably castrating you as well. However, in due course, some senior officer appeared and led us for several miles to where we were supposed to be, and we took up positions on the reverse slope of a small narrow valley.

We were there a few days and unfortunately the Germans quickly had the exact range of the valley, although it was out of their view. I suppose they knew well enough we were there and only had to read it off a map. A driver was wounded in the foot at my troop headquarters: I didn't take his boot off because I felt it was probably holding the foot together. The 88mm was a very nasty weapon, because it had a very high muzzle velocity and the shell arrived before the sound. Psychologically this was very disturbing; one could not brace oneself for the explosion.

A lot of damage was being done by one particular Tiger tank, and the colonel decided that under cover of night we would put two anti-tank guns on the forward slope for a day, comparatively close to the German lines. The Tiger had a habit of popping its turret up above the ridge on which the Germans were, firing and then withdrawing. Our guns were to remain dug in, camouflaged, nobody moving, until the Tiger appeared, and then to get it. My troop was chosen to provide one of the two guns – Sergeant Davies was nominated and I was to meet the colonel with the gun at midnight.

As usual it was black as your hat. I can remember to this day waking up every ten minutes, afraid I should not be at the rendezvous at the right time to meet the colonel. I was, of course, and he and I led the gun down to where he wanted it. Davies and his gun team then had until dawn to get dug in and camouflage themselves. At daybreak I

I opened my eyes to see a German helmet over me outlined against the dark sky, and a Schmeisser sub-machine gun pressing hard into my stomach. I withdrew my hands from my blankets and raised them over my head. The voice said: "Get op!"

hardly needed glasses to spot them, and I thought they looked rather conspicuous, but no German fire descended upon them. Unfortunately, the Tiger never showed its head that day and they didn't get a shot in.

In due course the Jerry was pushed back, and on 30th April we moved forward on to the Goubellat plain. My guns were set out at 200 yard intervals and there were no infantry, but a detachment of four heavy machine gunners of the Northumberland Fusiliers. Opposite us, a couple of miles away, the German line was held by the Hermann Goering Division of the SS, who had the reputation of not taking prisoners. We were, I suppose, very exposed, but there was no enemy fire whatever. We were only 30 miles from Tunis, the enemy was retreating and we had enormous confidence. I went to bed that night in my pyjamas, for the first time since we left Tmimi, as a kind of celebration. The gods were waiting to strike!

Here Rene Hiller, a friend in another battery, hit a mine in his Jeep and was so badly wounded he was invalided back to England. There he was encouraged to cycle to strengthen his injured leg, was knocked off his bicycle by a car and killed! His sister was Dame Wendy Hiller, the Academy Award winning actress of screen and stage, and there was a tremendously strong family facial resemblance.

It was 1st May. I made my troop headquarters centrally between my guns, with four men of the Northumberland Fusiliers to provide the guard, and went to bed on the back of my 15 cwt truck. At some time in the middle of the night I was awakened by something pressing hard into my stomach, and a low voice hissing: "Hands op!"

I opened my eyes to see a German helmet over me outlined against the dark sky, and a Schmeisser sub-machine gun pressing hard into my stomach. I withdrew my hands from my blankets and raised them over my head. The voice said: "Get op!"

Now I was lying in bed with the blankets firmly fastened beneath me (I cannot remember how) and I found it impossible to raise myself without putting my hands down

At that point there was a burst of machine gun fire and I learned later that they had shot dead the four Northumberland Fusiliers, all lying in their blankets – some guard!

to heave myself up, and every time I tried to do this the Jerry officer said "Hands op" again and pressed his gun even more fiercely in my rib.

I expostulated: I doubt if he understood, but the third time I insisted and fortunately he did not shoot. I got out of the back of the truck, insisted in putting on my shoes and boots and found they had also got my driver, Lawton. At that point there was a burst of machine gun fire and I learned later that they had shot dead the four Northumberland Fusiliers, all lying in their blankets – some guard!

At least it emphasised that, unarmed as I was, it was wiser not to argue. The lieutenant handed Lawton and me over to two privates to start a march back to the German lines some two miles away. It was very dark, and I thought hard about making a run for it, but the Schmeisser which one of the Germans carried was a very effective weapon, and I doubted if I could get out of sight and reach before he could use it. So we plodded through the darkness. After about an hour I was led into a tent to confront a company commander who politely enquired in English if I was wounded.

On being told I was not, Lawton and I were let into a large and well dug-in defence post containing a number of Germans including a sergeant major who had lived in Singapore for many years and spoke perfect English. He boastfully spoke of the Germans winning the war, which was a pretty good example of their morale, since it could not be more than a few weeks before they were defeated in Africa. However, as I have said, they were a crack division of the SS. I made a bet with him, to be kept after the war, that we should win, and I wrote down his name and address in Hamburg. Just two years later I arrived in Hamburg to join a new regiment on VE day: the street, indeed the whole area where he had lived, was no more – it was flat.

1943 (2ND MAY)

Lawton and I in the morning were passed on to a smallish tent which appeared to be a battalion office, with a corporal clerk working behind a trestle table. We sat or lay on the ground most of the day, and I was fascinated to observe that every time a private soldier came into the office he came smartly to attention, gave the Nazi salute and a "Heil Hitler!" before giving his message or whatever to the man behind the table.

All this to a corporal! In the British Army the most he would have received would have been a casual "watcher, corp!" Afternoon came and we were led to a motorcycle combination; the Germans used a lot of these. With a German rider, Lawton in the sidecar and me on the pillion, we drove most of the way to Tunis then marched the last few miles, along with some other dispirited British prisoners. I was handed over to be interrogated and found myself seated and offered a cigarette by a German intelligence officer.

You may give only name, rank and number if captured, so this is what I did. He knew my division, the 1st Armoured, because of the shoulder flash on my shirt, of a white rhino, known to all as the Pregnant Pig. So he diverted to the line that the Germans and the British should be on the same side, both fighting the Russians. I was happy to argue with him about this, but he soon found he was getting nowhere so quickly dropped his mask of pleasantness, and I was dismissed. I had now, of course, been separated from Lawton who was with the rest of the other ranks and I found myself confined in two rooms of a school in Tunis, with a number of other officers, mostly British, some American.

We were given a meal of soup in a large dixie, not the easiest thing to deal with minus a spoon or mess tin. However, an American officer solved the problem by removing the leather padding from inside his steel helmet

TAKEN PRISONER ...AND CUT ADRIFT

which he then used as a soup bowl, and we shared it. Seeing me standing with one foot at right angles to the other, and my knee slightly bent (as was my habit) he deduced I must be a fencer. I had reluctantly to disillusion him.

What worried me now was that I was imprisoned, idle and with nothing to read. To my delight the second room contained a large shelf of French paperback books, and my reading French being pretty good I was able to pick out three likely looking ones and stuff them under my shirt. Some slight disquiet was also caused by the information soon passed from one to another that officer prisoners of war were being flown back to Italy as quickly as possible, but that three out of four planes making the passage were shot down by our aircraft.

Our temporary incarceration in the school did not last long. We were transported to a disused factory on the main road into Tunis from the south. We could wander about it quite freely, but a detailed inspection revealed no apparent means of escape. We were now in Italian hands, and there were two Italian armed guards outside on the road. For the next few days I ate the miserable meals provided, read my French novels, and for the first time in my life found myself dying to smoke. The Italian guards did very well out of our lack of cigarettes: they charged the equivalent of ten shillings a packet of shocking Italian cigarettes, at a time when English ones were a shilling a packet. Fortunately I had a few French francs with me.

On the morning of 7th May we decided that something was happening in the world outside.

1943 (7TH MAY)

We were able to look out at the street through barred windows at the front, and from early morning there seemed to be a great deal of army traffic coming into the town from the south, from the direction of the country. About midday it slackened off, then ceased altogether, and the street was empty. Suddenly at 3.15pm a German armoured car came pelting down the road carrying a soldier in the turret, armed with a gun. It says something for the state of feeling between the Germans and Italians that he blasted off with his Schneisser at our two guards.

One fell dead and the one at the door was wounded in the thigh. We pulled him inside and edged outside onto the pavement to await events. It had been the last retreating German vehicle, and in about 15 minutes we saw tanks and armoured cars coming down the road – 11th Hussars from the 8th Army

Suddenly at 3.15pm a German armoured car came pelting down the road carrying a soldier in the turret, armed with a gun. It says something for the state of feeling between the Germans and Italians that he blasted off with his Schneisser at our two guards.

I drove on to the battery position to see Sergeant Major Thomas walking along, wearing my cord trousers. In traditional fashion my possessions, other than strictly personal, had been divided. "Get those trousers off, sergeant major" I shouted from my truck window.

and Derbyshire Yeomanry from the 1st Army. As they came up we yelled ourselves hoarse: I literally jumped up and down: we were beside ourselves with joy.

I suppose I then walked off down the road, the main Avenue De Bardo leading into the city. In almost no time the streets were packed with shouting, cheering French men and women. My hand was shaken a hundred times, girls kissed me and fathers invited me to a meal. Eventually I accepted an invitation and had an excellent meal surrounded by an admiring family.

Next morning I found where the town major had established his office and enquired if he knew where the 76th Anti-Tank were. He said all ex-prisoners must report to a special transit camp. There was obviously a strong risk one might be sent as reinforcement to any unit, so privately I had not the slightest intention of going near it. However, meanwhile he asked me to go and take over a German military hospital until the RAMC could arrive to do so. So I walked there, sending a looting Arab into paralysed terror on the way. He was not sure if I might shoot him, although I was in fact unarmed.

Arriving at the hospital I was politely greeted and I informed them I was in charge. They gave me a Luger pistol, saying they had no idea how it had got there (!) and I had it long after. I dined that night with the German doctors, and found it a very pleasant occasion. I was given a private room and bed and was able to borrow a razor and suchlike.

Next morning an RAMC doctor arrived and took over, and I set off into the street to find a vehicle. There were plenty of abandoned German vehicles about, and I soon found a fitter's truck with the key in the ignition. I pressed the starter button and it instantly burst into life! It would make a wonderful caravan, rather like a small sized furniture van, and the back was empty except for a chest, full of beautiful fitter's tools. My next task was to find out where my regiment had got to. I knew that the fighting had moved out towards Cap Bon, to the east, so I set off in that direction, periodically enquiring for the 76th Anti-tank or the 1st Armoured Division, when I found some likely British unit to ask. No one seemed to have heard of them, and I was sometimes viewed with some suspicion.

As I got near our forward units I came under German shellfire and took temporary shelter in a ditch. When it finished I went on and found some British who themselves said they had been about to shoot me up, not unnaturally, when they saw a German truck, presumably containing Germans, coming along the road. However, at last someone had an idea of where the regiment was, and late in the afternoon of 8th May I drove on to

TAKEN PRISONER ...AND CUT ADRIFT

the battery position to see Sergeant Major Thomas walking along, wearing my cord trousers. In traditional fashion my possessions, other than strictly personal, had been divided. "Get those trousers off, sergeant major" I shouted from my truck window – to his intense astonishment. They were quickly returned, and I learned I had been posted missing, believed taken prisoner. Days later Lawton, my driver, got back, having come through the official channels.

Everyone welcomed me, and Dick Hockin commented that while I had always been thin I now looked like a skeleton. True, there had been little for me to eat for a week and I'd had a good deal to worry about. My first task was to send a telegram home saying words to the effect of "safe and well – ignore previous telegram." This assumed the War Office would have sent my family a telegram, but it turned out later that they had not, since Army machinery worked rather slowly. So my mother and father were somewhat puzzled on receiving my telegram - but happy.

1943 (MAY-DECEMBER)
CHAPTER 11

A TIME TO INDULGE
...COMING TO TERMS WITH PEACE

A TIME TO INDULGE ...COMING TO TERMS WITH PEACE

On 10th May 1943 the German and Italian armies in Africa surrendered, and that was the last fighting I ever did, though I was to serve in the Army for another three years. However, there were plenty more interesting experiences to come.

Looking back on the African campaign, I had been in it from beginning to end, and had taken part in a least six major battles. I had been among the few to serve under Wavell in the earlier days, and under Monty for the last period. I was in the siege of Tobruk from beginning to end. I was captured by the Germans and released by our own army six days later. I was often short of water, and had diarrhoea almost permanently for three years. All in all, the most eventful period of my life.

I now had a four and a half gallon jerrican of wine, a looted truck and a peaceful existence. I felt pleased that Monty was not the only one to have his own caravan, but in about ten days the order came down from group headquarters to hand in all captured vehicles, so reluctantly I had to part with it. I then built myself a square pavilion, made from a vast piece of captured German canvas, where I lived quite happily. I used to practise firing my Luger at an empty wine bottle set up in the gully behind my tent, and improved my marksmanship considerably. I had taken care to collect a large stock of 9mm ammunition.

The only other thing I can recall about this period is a large regimental party, at which somebody had fashioned a lethal cocktail mixture of which I only had a few, then passed out - the only time this has ever happened to me. I think it must have been now, in the midsummer, I experienced the greatest heat I can recall. The thermometer rose to 128°F and all work was suspended for all ranks for three days while it lasted. I tried to fry an egg on a metal sheet in full sun, but without success.

Before long we moved into Algeria, a distance of about 500 miles, and settled in a vineyard at Sidi Moussa, some 15 miles inland from Algiers. We knew, I think, that the Army would shortly invade Sicily and Italy, as Churchill had been talking about the soft underbelly of Europe for long enough –

Looking back on the African campaign, I had been in it from beginning to end, and had taken part in a least six major battles.

it was not so soft! However, although we did not know it, we were not to take part. There was now a regimental re-organisation of which I cannot recall the details, except that I was posted to a new battery, 199 Battery. It was commanded by Vere Margesson, a Rhodesian, and a very casual character indeed.

Rhodesia was a tiny country at this time and had formed a volunteer anti-tank battery, which Vere had joined. He was pretty old for active service in the ranks, about 40; indeed he had a son in the Navy, aged 18 – Stoker Margesson. He had gone to OCTU in Cairo in the early days and he told how he was called for preliminary interview with the CO, who said "Ah, Margesson – unusual name. Any relation to Capt. Margesson, the Minister for War?" "My brother, sir." "Ah" – pause – "I don't think you'll find much difficulty with this course, Margesson…" Vere's older brother was indeed Churchill's Minister for War at the time. Wyrley Birch, our Rhodesian colonel, tended to collect Rhodesian officers.

At this time also, Arthur Canfor joined us as battery captain, a friendly sandy haired man. Apart from Vere he was the only other married officer in the battery: indeed very few of us in the regiment altogether were married. Arthur and his wife Jean both became solicitors and Vivienne and I stayed with them in Molesey after the war.

Following the end of the African campaign the division was to be re-equipped, and I was fortunate enough to be the officer nominated by 199 Battery to go down to Cairo to fetch back new vehicles. Most supplies and reinforcements had till now made the long journey round the Cape, stopping at Durban en route. By this time the great bulk of people in the forces had come via Durban, and their tales of the hospitality they enjoyed there made me green with envy. Vast numbers of South Africans of British descent apparently used to line the quay there when a ship came in and sweep people off to their luxurious blonde daughters. That was the tale anyway.

Since we invaded Sicily in July and the Italian mainland in September 1943 the Mediterranean became much more open, but the fact remained that these vast supplies of vehicles which were wanted to re-equip the divisions in Algeria were stuck 3,000 miles away in Cairo, having come round the Cape. They would no doubt have started the trip when Tunisia and Algeria were still in enemy hands.

Those from the other three batteries were Dick Hockin, David Matthias and Nick Smith, all friends of mine, and we were to take about 100 men to bring back 100 vehicles by road, 2,750 miles from Cairo to Algiers. We embarked on what had been a P&O ship for a luxurious voyage down to Alexandria: I say luxurious because the meals were excellent and in the mess each table for four had its own waiter, so service was immediate and deferential. Day after day we idled on deck in the hot August sun. Arriving at Alexandria we entrained for Cairo and installed our troops at Abbassia barracks. We were supposed to stay there ourselves, but since we had had no leave for over a year we were going to make the most of the five days we were told we should have until our vehicles were ready.

We found a large room for four at the National Hotel in Sharia Suliman Pasha, and for a few days we spent madly. It then transpired the vehicles would not be ready for some time; our five days turned into five weeks in Cairo. We survived financially only because David Matthias was able to con the pay office into paying us something called "detention allowance." Permanently living in a hotel was expensive, apart from drinking and dining out every night, and going everywhere by taxi. After issuing my cheque for a week's hotel bill on our last day I had to visit Barclays to request an overdraft to meet it.

But to go back, our life developed into pleasant routine. Mid-morning coffee and

1943, Sidi Moussa Mess, Arthur Canfor, Tom Rogers, Hock, DGM, Bill, Vere Margesson, Sheila

delicious cake at Groppi's Cafe, lunchtime drinks in a bar, afternoon beside the pool at the Gezira Club and in the evenings either more drinks or a cinema, or dancing at Groppi's Garden. There were 20 cinemas, most of them with English and American films. Gezira Club occupied Gezira Island in the Nile and was a country club run on racist lines – no Egyptians. Squash and other games were available, but we concentrated on the pool, beside which one sat, John Collins in hand, diving in every now and then to cool off. Our group often included two ENSA girls, because one of them, Avril Angers, was infatuated with David Ross. David was tall, fair, good looking and very attractive to women. Avril Angers, we occasionally used to see years later on British television.

Dancing at Groppi's Garden I have already described when I was at OCTU. When I did not dine in our own hotel I usually went to the Continental, which was pretty free of senior officers. They used to congregate at Shepheards, as did all the other base-wallahs, whom we despised.

Our favourite bar was the Ex-Morandi, a small establishment kept by a white Russian called Jean. It was the Rhodesian centre in Cairo, their invariable meeting point, and Jean was a master of cocktails, of which there was an extensive list. Most nights two or three of us would call to sample a series of delicious and potent cocktails, with Jean sticking each bill on a spike. At evening's end one just asked for the total and paid: Jean appeared to be scrupulously honest. He was also brilliant at skimming the glass along the bar to stop in front of you. So close did our association with Jean become that when he got married in September the bar was closed to the public the night before and open only to his regular friends, all drinks free.

Nick Smith was the senior officer in our group and he arranged for the sergeant in charge of the party to call at the hotel regularly for orders, if any. We held a weekly pay parade in the Ezbekieh Gardens, sitting on a park seat and dishing out each man's pay packet to the queue.

I met various people in the bars I visited. Among the Americans was Milton J. Marx, a journalist on the Stars & Stripes forces newspaper. I read subsequently that the Marx brothers had another brother called Milton, who did not join them in films: I have sometimes wondered if this was the man. Another American was Chapin Leinback, a diplomat at their embassy whom I go to know quite well. A soft-spoken intellectual, he was quite entertaining company. His mother had a villa at Cassis in the south of France, to which I was invited after the war.

David and I often used to see a man around the bars who always seemed somewhat cocky and aggressive. He was a pilot who had been shot up while coming down on a parachute from his crashing plane. One night in his cups he confessed that his penis had been shot off. David and I, also in our cups, insisted on taking him down to the loos to see if he was telling the truth. He was. Thereafter we sympathised with his moods, and promised not to tell the girl he was taking out.

I once visited the third-floor flat of some acquaintance. The room was crowded with people and I picked up his cat to stroke it. The animal took one spring from my arms straight out of the open window. I had the embarrassing task of reporting this event to my host, who was, needless to say, particularly fond of the cat. He rushed downstairs – three flights – to search the area of the garden just below but could not find it. It must have crawled into the bushes but I could not see how it could survive.

One day, coming back to the hotel at lunchtime with a cheer on, the four of us were stopped by an Arab with a sack who asked us if we wanted to buy a snake. I felt a snake was just what I wanted at the time, so he opened the sack full of writhing creatures and withdrew one about 30 inches long. I paid him, tied it in a knot around my wrist and we continued along the street, discussing what we were to call it. Since it was David's birthday we were celebrating, and his name was David Wyndham Lyner Matthias, we christened it Wyndham. Wyndham, on my wrist, was quite unperturbed, and I handled him (or her) with complete confidence and we returned to the hotel and put him in my bedside cupboard.

Next morning I thought I had better warn the chambermaid so I showed her Wyndham in the cupboard. She gave a shriek and fled. The manager arrived, and we arranged that the chambermaid would continue to clean the room, but give the cupboard a wide berth. I ordered some milk in a saucer and tried to get Wyndham to take it: he would not, and bit me. At this point I wondered if he was poisonous: I was obviously now, when sober, handling him with much less confidence. I kept him several days, then one day found his cupboard empty. We searched the room without success and decided not to mention his escape to the manager. A day or two more elapsed, then coming back at lunchtime as usual we saw a great crowd outside the hotel.

Fighting our way to the front, we saw two Arabs beating a poor little snake to death with sticks! We slipped quietly inside the hotel, deciding that Wyndham must have slithered down creeper that covered the outside wall after getting out of our window.

David discovered an excellent and purely Egyptian restaurant in what was, I believe, an area out of bounds to the British. We went there several times, always receiving much bowing from the proprietor, who referred to David as "the young fair prince," and indeed to me as "the young dark prince." We usually had what we called squashed pigeon (it was boned) and the knife and fork always appeared to be flung down on the table as an afterthought. The pudding was always very sweet, often something similar to shredded wheat soaked in syrup.

It was all great fun, but at last the day came when we went with our men to collect our vehicles from the ordnance depot. Everybody else in the division had gone back long before: being fashionable cavalry regiments they got preference, if one can call it that. We decided it was ridiculous to have four officers to escort our convoy, and we divided into two groups of two. The movement order gave full details of exactly where we were to halt each day, which involved a daily journey of 100 miles. So it was arranged that Dick Hockin and David Matthias would make a dash for Tripoli, 1,400 miles away, while Nick Smith and I would bring the convoy on, taking a fortnight. Nick and I would then go on alone for a tour of Tunisia and Algeria, rejoining the convoy

1943, Sidi Moussa Mess, Arthur Canfor, Vere Margesson, Tom Rogers, DGM, Hock

shortly before Algiers.

The vehicles being brought included two staff cars, so we each had a staff car. The convoy we were in charge of actually included far more than our own 100 vehicles, for there were many other officers and men, chiefly returning to their units from hospital and so on, and also a detachment of American ambulance of the Friends Ambulance Unit. The whole journey would be 2,700 miles.

We set off up the coast road in our staff car leading the convoy at about 20mph. But since the movement order stipulated a departure time of 07:00 we had reached our day's destination by about lunchtime. After a couple of days of this, Nick called a conference of all officers and announced that instead of keeping Middle East Time all ranks on the convoy would keep Convoy Time, i.e. watches were put back two hours. So instead of having to get up at first light we rose when the sun was comfortably up, and finished the day's journey at a convenient time in mid-afternoon instead of lunchtime, yet the hours in the movement order (of which others had copies) were strictly adhered to.

A few conservative souls tut-tutted, but it was actually an excellent idea, and worked admirably, since we had no contact with anybody else working on standard time. Since the war in Africa had finished, the whole area for the next 2,000 miles was virtually empty, except for the odd fuel depot and ration depot, as everybody was up in Algeria.

Nick and I soon decided it was a waste of time trundling along at the head of the convoy so we would often go ahead to recce

Nick called a conference of all officers and announced that instead of keeping Middle East Time all ranks on the convoy would keep Convoy Time, i.e. watches were put back two hours. So instead of having to get up at first light we rose when the sun was comfortably up.

the site of the night's camp, make arrangements for refuelling and rations, and so on. We also took the opportunity to divert to see the Roman cities of Apollonia and Leptis Magna. Apollonia occupied a marvellous site among the hills east of Benghazi, on a shelf overlooking the sea. Backed by green hills, there was this vast city on a flat shelf, miles from anywhere, empty of people.

Leptis Magna, nearer Tripoli, was not so remarkable a site, but more remarkable in its state of preservation, buried by sand for nearly 1,500 years. The Italians had achieved a great feat in excavating it. Nick and I wandered around, utterly alone, viewing temples, the theatre, the market place with stone tables, the quay of the port with steps and bollards. Particularly striking, since it brought daily life so close, was the public lavatory with stone seats round the inside of three walls of the large room and running water below.

Between these two cities lay the border between Cyrenaica and Tripolitania, marked by Marble Arch, beside which we camped for the night. This was a great building, rather like the Arc de Triomphe spanning the road. Mussolini had built it to commemorate his conquest of Libya and it had an internal staircase to the top. As our convoy started off next morning Nick and I climbed to the top, 90 feet up, and watched the vehicles pass beneath far below.

At last we reached Tripoli, declared a rest day for maintenance, and joined up with Dick and David, who had had a pleasant stay with Dick's brother. They had discovered and been made welcome at the YWCA (not the residential part) and for two days we all four went there for tea or coffee. I have the pleasantest memories of sitting in a little courtyard at the back, in great heat, under a pomegranate tree, and picking pomegranates while drinking coffee.

Nick and I then set off on our expedition, deep inland into Tunisia and Algeria. We were in the staff car, followed by a 15 cwt truck with two men carrying supplies of fuel and rations and a tent.

Throughout the journey from Alexandria, whenever we had been near enough to the sea we had gone for a swim and a long bask in the sun. We always, of course, swam naked since there had never been a woman near in the hundreds of times I had been swimming in nearly four years since I landed in Palestine. But a day's journey after visiting Sabratha, our third Roman city, we turned inland and headed for the Holy City of Kairouan, a major place of Muslim pilgrimage. Outside the walls we walked through a street of mud huts, with an open sewer running down a gully in

Throughout the journey from Alexandria, whenever we had been near enough to the sea we had gone for a swim and a long bask in the sun.

the middle, producing a powerful stench for a considerable distance. Within the walls we looked longingly at the Great Mosque, but were not allowed to enter: we were, after all, the only infidels in Kairouan at the time. We bought some little cooked sausages from a street vendor, which were extremely tasty.

We drove on towards Le Kef, and were able to shoot a wild duck and, by chance, to knock down a rabbit on the road. There was a fine dinner that night, and in case marauding Arabs had seen our fire we moved about a mile away without lights after dark before pitching camp. Next day near Le Kef we decided to test out French hospitality and called at a country house farm, where we were received with open arms and asked to stay to dinner. We were given an admirable meal of several courses - French cooking at its best - and were able to offer our thanks by leaving a few tins of cigarettes.

We drove through vast areas of hills covered in cork forests. Sometimes we would see charcoal burners at work, with a great dome of sticks about 20 feet across and a wisp of smoke issuing from the top. One afternoon we camped and sat drinking wine and entered into a bet between us about climbing a mountain, which was a pyramid filling the skyline. We ultimately set off in the early evening taking each a water bottle, a minimum of food and a blanket, telling the two drivers to wait until we came back.

We had not got far before night fell so there was nothing for it but to bed down in the wood where we found ourselves and wrap ourselves each in our blanket. It was terribly cold towards dawn, but at daybreak we decided to fulfil our promise and went on, steering by the sight of the peak ahead. When we could see it, that is, because we were crossing the grain of the land and had to keep climbing ridges and then down again into the valley beyond. In one of these valleys we came across a native village where an Arab showed us the marks where a wild boar had been rooting in the crops.

As we climbed the steep slope of the mountain beyond we heard something crash about in the wood on our left – perhaps a boar. We reached the top in early afternoon, hungry, because our food had run out, but triumphant. It was about 4,000 feet. We had carefully noted our outward route across country, and were able to find our way back, finally coming into sight of our car and truck at 6pm as dusk was falling, over 24 hours since our departure. The drivers had been worried, but sensibly had not shifted.

This was not the only time we were hungry, because a few days later we ran out of food before we could reach anywhere that we could draw rations. We camped in the cork forest and found beef-steak fungi, and having fried them had to subsist until next day when we were able to drive north to the main road and restock.

We reached the top in early afternoon, hungry, because our food had run out, but triumphant. It was about 4,000 feet.

A TIME TO INDULGE ...COMING TO TERMS WITH PEACE

1943-44 (OCTOBER)
CHAPTER 12

SEEING THE SIGHTS
...AND PARADING WITH A FOUR-LEGGED FRIEND

We rejoined the main convoy somewhere near Constantine in Algeria, a place lying athwart a deep gorge which later reminded me of Luxembourg. Shortly before Algiers, we had a final rest day for maintenance, and at my urging the four of us drove back some distance to where I had seen a striking pyramidal mountain, of about 6,000 feet. We were at some height before we left the car and started the climb, having crossed a bridge over a wide river. We reached the top and found an extensive view, but also just over the other slope was a man ploughing who rather put us to shame. It started to rain, and as we came down we became soaked to the skin, so when we reached the river instead of walking round by the bridge we plunged straight in. In our clothes it was quite warm, and the fast current swept us downstream, but we easily swam across.

My final recollection of the journey is of the four of us driving off on a detour through the hills and forests. We were in a staff car, wearing our Hebron (sheepskin) long coats and smoking cigars. We also halted to broach some wine. It seemed the acme of luxury … I was 25.

We settled in our vineyard in Sidi Moussa. Our quarters were not terribly good compared with those of many other units; they had large requisitioned country houses. But at least the officers had a row of individual tents, with a larger tent for a mess and a charming little single storey cottage as an ante-room.

There was also a maize field alongside so we had corn on the cob – it was October. Grapes from the vines were small, green and sour, not much good for eating. The sergeant cook in charge of the men's cookhouse was brilliant, but we had to make do with L/Bdr Bratt, who was not very clever, but willing. Arthur Canfor used to march in the mess at teatime and so often demand a six egg omelette (eggs hereabout were very small) that I had to start charging them to his mess bill. We had to buy eggs from the local Arabs, and they were quite expensive. I knew – I was mess secretary.

The regiment was re-organised as the 64th Anti-Tank, and Vere decided the simple designation 199 Battery was too plain. Like my old South Notts Hussars, units with any pretensions had some title such as 107th (SNH) Regiment, RHA so tongue in cheek we christened ourselves 199 (FNT) Battery RA, and stuck up a sign at our camp entrance to publicise it. When asked what FNT stood for, we replied: "Fairly near two hundred," but in fact it can be guessed that F– was the normal army adjective. Only someone like a Rhodesian, with a Rhodesian commanding officer, could have got away with it. Shortly afterwards the commanding officer Wyrley Birch left us, and he had to leave his dog behind. She was a dachshund bitch, and as

My final recollection of the journey is of the four of us driving off on a detour through the hills and forests. We were in a staff car, wearing our Hebron (sheepskin) long coats and smoking cigars.

most dogs in the regiment were named after the place they were acquired, she was called Trips - short for Tripoli. She took a fancy to me and used to insist on coming on parade with me, which was awkward, but she was very affectionate. While we were in Algeria she had nine puppies, just like shelling peas, and when she had finished she jumped out of her box and ran proudly around the room wagging her tail.

The new colonel had already been with us for some months as second in charge, Harding-Newman by name. A little, strutting man with a monocle, he was always referred to as – Hardly Human. He was not popular among junior officers, and he did not care for the 8th Army style of dress of corduroy trousers, a jersey and suede boots.

My recollections of the next few months nearly all centre on social life. I think it must have been here I took out two or three times a nurse of the Queen Alexandra's Imperial Nursing Service. I remember nothing about her except that my driver Jones once referred to her memorably as "that stout piece." Rather unfair, I thought.

Local wine, brandy and liqueurs were good, unlimited and cheap. A favourite with us was champagne cocktails, made of sparkling white wine and brandy. We held parties in our cottage, to one of which we had all the regimental officers and also local French ladies. These grass widows were the wives of Vichy French officers who were interned, and they were only too willing for an affair. I was doing famously with an attractive woman and made an assignation, only to find the colonel starting to pay her marked attention.

I regretfully withdrew (a) because I was not too popular with the colonel anyway, and (b) because she would presumably gain far more social cachet from an affair with a colonel than with a mere subaltern. She did have an affair with him, and detailed accounts of his visits to her house were passed back through the grapevine of the other women, who all used to discuss their lovers. Dick Hockin struck up an acquaintance with a lady which ripened into a fully blown affair. She lived in Algiers some 15 miles away, and he, having no Jeep at the time, was known to visit her in a portee (a gun-tower 3 ton lorry) which he parked outside her house all night.

That winter every regiment in the division held a dance. The armoured regiments were all old cavalry regiments – The Queen's Bays, 9th Lancers and 10th Hussars. The 10th Hussars' dance was held in a large room in a country house which was their headquarters, and they had engaged a band from a nearby American unit. There were about 15 of them, mostly Black, and they took up nearly half the room: the noise in such a small space was earsplitting. I noticed the squadron daily orders posted up outside, signed by Major the Earl of ......, detailing Lieut, Lord ...... as orderly officer and so on.

A tale circulated also about one of the squadron commanders "doing a Uriah" – (see 2 Samuel, Chapter II). Before leaving the UK, he had apparently walked off with the wife of one of his troop commanders, and the latter had then been killed in action in Africa. To quote The Bible, King David had said to his general: "Set ye Uriah in the forefront of the hottest battle, and retire ye from him, that he may be smitten, and die."

Towards Christmas the regiment acquired a flock of turkeys, on the hoof, and a turkey keeper was appointed. Turkeys are notoriously delicate and temperamental, and our turkey man had no experience of them. Some died, and the rest seemed to get thinner and thinner, so while we did get turkey on Christmas Day it was a pretty small portion.

We used to go into Algiers city occasionally, but the Medina was out of bounds, and there was little to do. At the Aletti, the best hotel, the route to the ladies' toilets lay through the gentlemen's urinal, which struck me as somewhat odd and not a little French.

Some time after Christmas an epidemic broke out of night time thefts from the officers' tents, which were pitched on the edge of our encampment overlooking a maize field. Several people were robbed and I felt sure that my turn would be next, so on retiring to bed I lay awake for an hour or two to see if anything happened. It didn't on the first night, but on the second night I saw a silhouette appear in the gap of the open tent flap.

I quietly reached for my Luger from beneath my pillow but could not be sure whether it was an Arab or a British soldier. I had to be sure, and slowly started to sit up. Alarmed, he turned to flee and I could clearly see he was in Arab dress. I leapt out of bed and, outside the tent, could just see him disappear in the darkness, fleeing across the field. I fired a couple of shots at him without effect: I tramped out over the field to see if I had by any chance hit him. At any rate, the robberies stopped.

In January 1944 the divisional commander decided to hold a vast, fortnight-long exercise for the whole division, and we all moved lock, stock and barrel into mountains some 50 miles south of Algiers. It was bitterly cold; we were sleeping in tents; and I contracted sinus sufficiently severe to send me to bed. That evening I started on a bottle of whisky, and as it went down the pain lessened. Nick visited me and helped a little, but basically I drank it myself and when only a quarter of the bottle remained, my pain had disappeared and I fell asleep. It was back next morning, I agree, but less severe.

The weather, as I say, was very bad, and it snowed, so the tanks found it difficult to move and the only part of the exercise I remember was a river crossing. The tanks drove across what was supposed to be a shallow spot and I followed in my Jeep. But the river was in flood after heavy rain. I got halfway across, revving hard, with the water up to the floor, and then I momentarily stuck. This was enough to stall the engine and the river flooded through, covering me up to the thighs. I had to be towed out by a tank.

It seemed a pity to miss the chance of climbing a mountain so I went off to the colonel to ask for three days' leave for a climbing expedition. The Army, always being keen on any sporting activity, granted my request. We had only army boots, and no rope, so the night before our departure I swarmed up one of the guy ropes which held a main pole of the marquee serving as our regimental mess. I cut off one of the other guys and hoped the tent wouldn't fall down. Thus equipped, we set off next morning in a 3 ton truck, taking with us a tent and plenty of food and fuel. We were heading for the biggest mountain I could find, Ras ed Timedonine, 2,305 metres tall in the Dzebel Djurdjura, the coastal range thereabouts of the Atlas mountains.

That's about 7,500 feet, and from the town of Bouira we drove steadily upwards, partly through forest, until we reached the snowline,

We were heading for the biggest mountain I could find, Ras ed Timedonine, 2,305 metres tall in the Dzebel Djurdjura, the coastal range thereabouts of the Atlas mountains.

at perhaps 5,500 feet. We made camp and I slept in the tent, Nick outside: I found him frost-covered in the morning, but quite warm beneath a sheepskin coat. We were into snow straightaway and followed the line of the road as far as we could, then up a gully onto a ridge. Here we turned right and climbed a ridge gently sloping upward, and heading for the peak. Fortunately it was a clear, bright day, with the pyramidal summit sticking out of a ring of cloud surrounding the slopes below it. Our route, however, lay across frozen snow, sloping to what looked like a precipice on our left, so we roped up, though our army boots were terribly unsuitable.

However, we avoided slipping, as we also did when we reached steeper rocks providing an easy scramble. All the while on this ridge we could see a parallel ridge about a mile away across a valley on our right, on which we could see what seemed to be animals moving. This seemed odd until we suddenly realised what they were – Barbary apes! They are the same as those on the Rock of Gibraltar, and of course this was the Barbary coast. My book on mammals says their habitat is rocky country, and sure enough we could now see them capering on the very summit of the rocky ridge.

We now entered the cloud, and on emerging found ourselves with a tremendous view of cloud below with the sun shining on it, just as from an aircraft, and rolling forested mountains beyond, many snow-covered. There wasn't another living soul for miles around, and we made our way safely down.

Next day we made our way up to the same ridge, this time turning left instead of right. Unlike the previous day we were in mist all the while but it was sufficiently bright to make the area, which had scattered contorted pine trees, look just like a Japanese print. What's more, with the faint sun behind us, and looking north, I could see thrown on the wall of mist in front of me a giant shadow of myself, surrounded by a circular rainbow. When I waved, the shadow waved, and I could see only my own shadow, not Nick's. I knew that this atmospheric phenomenon was known as the Spectre of the Brocken, and that it was very rare: years later I saw the same thing with my son Nick from the summit of Snowdon.

It began to snow, and in a few minutes

1944, Sheila and Bill

everything was blotted out. We had to head for home using a compass, with the ever present danger of coming down in the wrong valley. We began to get so tired and cold that we realised how easy it would be to give up under such conditions. However, we made it.

Next day we packed up and decided to take the truck further up the road, over the snow, to see if we could force a passage over the pass. We got quite a long way before we finally stuck in snow on the narrow road, with a cliff dropping away on our right. Although the road was blocked with snow, the extreme outside edge was clear.

There was no possibility of turning round, since the road was little more than the truck's width, so we had to back. To get a grip, this meant putting the outer wheels on the very edge of the road which was clear of snow, but the edge of the precipice. Nick took the driving seat and slowly backed round a curve while I directed him, and after about 200 yards we reached a place where, with extreme caution, we could turn. We headed back for camp.

The exercise over, we returned to Sidi Moussa. Spring came on, and Vere got to know a WRNS second officer by the name of Sheila. She was invited to dinner in the mess and came together with another second officer, Margaret Bannister, known as "Bill." As so often with pairs of girlfriends, one was much more attractive than the other, and in this case the attractive one was Bill. I promised to show her a camel and she agreed to come out with me on a picnic. We drove out in my Jeep into the mountains to where I had, in fact, recently seen a camel caravan. Thereafter Vere and I would meet Bill and Sheila every four days and go on a swan, usually to Sidi Ferrouch, a tiny village on the seashore some miles west of Algiers.

There we would swim and sunbathe then go for dinner in the one and only little restaurant. The meals were simple but quite good: food was difficult for them so the pudding course was invariably medlars, which presumably fruit early. Vere's friendship with Sheila was platonic, as she was conscious he was married. So was mine with Bill, through her wish rather than mine, but we all remained close friends for many months, and used to write to each other after we left for Italy.

Sometimes Dick or David would join us. For about a fortnight Algeria suffered from a plague of locusts. It was an extraordinary sight to see the air thick in every direction for miles with these green, two inch long, flying creatures. It was not bad enough for them to strip every plant, but no doubt they did a lot of damage. One day I went on a really long trip in a Jeep with another chap through the mountains and to the edge of the desert to the south.

In the barren hills bordering the desert we suddenly ran into a great cloud of locusts heading north. It was a vivid illustration of how they breed in the desert and migrate to fertile areas. Once, driving in the Jeep to Sidi Ferrouch with Bill and Sheila there was an agonized shriek from the back seat... a locust had flown up Bill's skirt – very shiver-making, but after the first cry she remained very cool.

David Matthias was at this time in a Battery, whose battery commander was Ronnie Crouch. Their party trick, when sufficient drink had been taken, was for David to stand with a cigarette in his lips while Ronnie stood six feet away with a riding whip and, with one slash, cut the cigarette in half. To see them do this, both swaying gently, was nerve wracking.

One day news arrived that Henry Freeman, the adjutant, had committed suicide. He was in deep trouble for having crashed his Jeep while drunk, after a general's order had been issued that officers must always take a driver when going out in the evening. It turned out he'd had wife trouble and had received a "Dear John" letter. Presumably the combination of these things had led him to retire to his tent and put a revolver bullet through his head. He was found by Dick Hockin. At the resultant court of inquiry it was, in the usual way, hushed up as an accident while cleaning his revolver. Sadly, none of us had realised he was in such a state of mind. I have known two men who committed suicide, and in neither case did

One day news arrived that Henry Freeman, the adjutant, had committed suicide. He was in deep trouble for having crashed his Jeep while drunk, after a general's order had been issued that officers must always take a driver when going out in the evening. It turned out he'd had wife trouble and had received a "Dear John" letter.

those around have the slightest idea of what was about to happen.

At about this time Nick Smith also left the regiment. He too had pranged his Jeep while far from sober and was posted to Palestine – and promptly promoted to captain. However, his unit soon joined in the Anzio landings, a very unpleasant business indeed. He survived, and we were next to meet in Brussels after the war, but before demob. We continued to correspond.

Nick was the only man I have ever known with whom I could talk happily, and from whom I could learn, on such a variety of subjects – English literature, poetry, war, birds, flowers, trees, country life, philosophy, sex, human nature, politics, horsemanship, farming and medicine. It was very refreshing in contrast to standard army chatter about personalities – "Do you know so and so, GSO 1 in 23rd Armoured Brigade – used to be brigade major of 2nd Armoured, etc. etc?"

On one of the final exercises before the division left for Italy, we all assembled on the bank of a wide river to watch a demonstration of a river crossing with tanks. The tanks were, of course, waterproofed and it was impressive to see a troop descend the bank, enter the river and steadily cross, with the water level just below the upper side of the tracks.

The first tank reached the other side at the appropriate spot and climbed out. Owing to the current, the second tank was carried further downriver, where the bank was steeper and obstructed with bushes. The tank scrabbled away, but failed to climb out, backed off and tried again, further down. Then it seemed to lose heart, or perhaps its engine stopped, and it was carried out into the middle of the river and swept rapidly down towards the sea. The last I saw of it was a pathetic object disappearing into the Mediterranean: I have often wondered how they got it back.

Nick was the only man I have ever known with whom I could talk happily, and from whom I could learn, on such a variety of subjects – English literature, poetry, war, birds, flowers, trees, country life, philosophy, sex, human nature, politics, horsemanship, farming and medicine.

1944 (JUNE)
CHAPTER 13
ONWARD TO ITALY
...AND EMBARRASSING BREAKFAST

ONWARD TO ITALY ...AND EMBARRASSING BREAKFAST

At the end of June the division left for Italy. Homes had to be found for the dogs. For example, 310 Battery had a bulldog called, inevitably, Winston: I do not know what happened to him - maybe he went over to Italy. He was a dog of great character who loved travelling in vehicles. He just used to hop into any vehicle near the mess and hope for a ride. I have known the time when I was halfway back from 310 to 199 (several miles apart) only to realise from stertorous breathing from behind that I was accompanied by Winston. As to Trips, I left her at the wrennery with Bill and Sheila, but only a month or two later they in turn were posted to Caserta just outside Naples. So Trips had to be handed over to another girl – all rather sad.

The regiment crossed the Mediterranean safely with no trouble from German submarines, and landed at Taranto. We anchored en route in the Grand Harbour at Valletta, which was packed with ships. Taranto had been badly bombed by us, being an important port for the Italian Navy, and it looked singularly depressing as Vere and I marched through it at the head of the battery.

I suppose we must have been marching somewhere to pick up transport, because we established ourselves in camp somewhere near Altamura, some 60 miles inland. The country was brown and barren, the villages dusty, dilapidated and utterly unpicturesque. I'd had high hopes of a beautiful country and thought wryly of Browning's lines:

Open my heart and you will see
Graved inside of it, "Italy"

However, I was to see a more attractive part of Italy later.

We were very isolated from anywhere interesting. Fifty miles in one direction was the Gulf of Taranto, where I went once to swim on a beautiful isolated beach. And fifty miles in the other was Bari, where I went once or twice with Dick Hockin to the officers club. En route we just skirted the Trulli country and on a bend was one single Trulli house, a little white round house with a conical roof painted with a strange symbol. The journey back at night in the dark along a winding hilly road was boring. I sat in the passenger's seat of

As to Trips, I left her at the wrennery with Bill and Sheila, but only a month or two later they in turn were posted to Caserta just outside Naples. So Trips had to be handed over to another girl – all rather sad.

the Jeep, which of course had no door, and used to doze off. As we swept round the right hand bends I used to start to fall out, but always woke up in time: fortunately one automatically does.

Vere was having an affair with, I think, a nurse whom he met in Bari, called Anne. One morning first thing I walked a few yards outside my tent in my pyjamas to spend a penny as one usually did and spotted Vere across the way doing the same thing. I called across a ribald remark, as did Dick, but Vere made frantic silencing gestures. Needless to say this only made us carry on, and not until we were all dressed did Vere come across and say he had Anne in the tent. We at once sent a message inviting her to breakfast: she felt embarrassed by then but came, and all was well.

Vere, as I say, was of good family and had been a young man about town in the 1920s. I imagine, really, he had been a bit of a black sheep, since he was sent out to farm in Rhodesia, at Umtali, in about 1927. In some ways he was rather like a character out of a PG Wodehouse novel. He used to refer to his uncle, the Earl of Buckingham, to whom he wrote quite frequently, as "My Uncle Bucks." He had no side whatever, and I take off my hat to him for volunteering for active service at the age of 40.

MEMOIRS OF A NOT TOO SERIOUS HUSSAR

1944 (AUGUST)
CHAPTER 14

LADY IN THE LEGION
...A MEMORABLE DINNER GUEST

While Vere was a passionate devotee of Vera Lynn, the rest of us preferred the American Forces Network. Tongue in cheek, we once sent a request, and during dinner a few nights later we suddenly heard – to our surprise – "Now here is a request, from Vere, Dick and Dennis of 199 Battery Royal Artillery. They say "We think your programme is the tops" and ask for "Queenie and Cutie." The full title of this favourite of ours was Queenie the Cutie of the Burlesque Show about a stripper, with a chorus which began "take it off, take it off…." One minute after it had finished the telephone rang. It was the adjutant, to say he thought it very poor publicity for the regiment. They must have been listening, anyway.

In early August we moved to an assembly area, which the regiment was in charge of to pass through the two French divisions for their invasion of Southern France. They were to sail from Taranto and they invaded on 15th August. We provided the tents, rationed them and so on. The few days before 15th August provided a remarkable experience, because we had with us a regiment of the Foreign Legion. Their ranks included about one third Africans and people of colour, and also, of course, Germans. All the officers were French except the intendant, an equivalent of lieutenant-quartermaster. They formed part of the force of General Koenig which had crossed the Sahara to Libya and fought at Bir Hacheim.

Their officers invited the officers of FNT to dinner, and I shall never forget sitting at trestle tables in an olive grove under the stars. Exceptionally, because she was English although not an officer, they invited a Miss Travers, who sat next to me: an English woman in the Foreign Legion! This remarkable woman had been living on the Riviera at the time France fell, and had escaped and joined the Free French forces as part of the Foreign Legion. It was the French custom to have women ambulance drivers, who operated between base hospitals and casualty clearing stations. But she was different.

She had driven across the Sahara, and been surrounded and under heavy enemy shellfire and infantry attacks for ten days at Bir Hacheim. Sometimes she had driven an ambulance, sometimes the breakdown wagon, sometimes other vehicles. Probably in her thirties, she might have been the daughter of the vicarage. And how she hated the Americans! The French had been fighting next to the Americans up in Northern Italy, and she bitterly condemned their softness, their unwillingness to do without supplies of doughnuts and ice cream, and what she considered their cowardice. We all felt this about them to a certain extent, at that time and in that theatre, but she was bitter.

After dinner we sat on the ground and

I shall never forget sitting at trestle tables in an olive grove under the stars. Exceptionally, because she was English although not an officer, they invited a Miss Travers, who sat next to me: an English woman in the Foreign Legion!

Susan Travers (23 September 1909 – 18 December 2003) was an Englishwoman who was the only woman to serve officially with the French Foreign Legion.

1944, Rome, St Peter's Basilica

sang. Like most other nations, the French could sing better than we, but we did our part. The very name Foreign Legion seemed romantic, and to be sitting there among them, laughing and drinking wine, the stars shining through the olives, to the sound of French songs, ah.....

Next morning Dick observed a legionnaire, bareheaded, being marched along under guard and asked a French officer what he had done. "Rape" was the reply. "What will happen to him?" "He will be shot," was the calm answer.

During the few days the French were with us I was in the officers club at Bari one night when a few French were there. Two or three of us thought it would be nice to sing the only French song we knew – Alouette. The English all promptly joined in, but the French were silent. We then learned that this seems to be a French Canadian song, so I quickly taught the simple words to a Foreign Legion major. He at once entered into the spirit, and standing on a chair conducted the whole company in the bar in a rousing rendering, with great panache.

In August I had three days' leave in Rome with a couple of others: it took ages to drive there by Jeep over twisting mountain roads. We passed Cassino, the hill still covered in our slit-trenches, completely overlooked by that beetling abbey above. Rome had been declared an open city and was unbombed. I recall seeing the Coliseum, the Spanish Steps and St Peter's. The Sistine Chapel was virtually empty, which would be quite impossible nowadays. I bought a dress length for my mother, which was difficult, since I neither knew what to buy nor how much, and my Italian was non-existent.

1944, Rome, below: Coliseum, right: Arch of Constantine

The division started to move up towards the Gothic line, and we found ourselves among low hills not far from the Adriatic coast near Ancona, south of Rimini. I was called to see the colonel to hear the news that I now qualified to come home to the UK – a posting, not merely leave – having been abroad five years (actually, by the time I got back it was about four years and ten months). I was given the choice: stay or go. I offered to stay, but my friends said I should be made to do so, so I accepted the offer.

A regimental mess party was held for my departure and, I believe, one other man whom I did not know. As usual on such occasions, thunderflashes were thrown. A thunderflash, used in battle training, is like an extremely loud firework, and to have one explode at one's heels with no warning is somewhat startling.

By 4th September the regiment was in action again, and I stayed back at regimental headquarters for a few days pending arrangements for my departure. I visited Porto Recanati, the little town on the coast a few miles away where Gigli, the famous tenor, originated, and saw his huge open air theatre. More interesting was Loreto, a famous Catholic place of pilgrimage. The church built as a shrine contains the Holy House, reputedly the home of the Virgin Mary miraculously transported from Nazareth, with a temporary stop in Yugoslavia, in the 13th Century. The Santa Casa itself is about the size of a large room and faced with elaborately carved marble, with which it was covered after its arrival. Beneath, the house is of brick, we are told. A more unlikely tale is difficult to imagine, and what I remember best are the magnificent bronze doors at the west end of the church.

I was bored at regimental headquarters and went to visit the battery with Arthur Canfor. We were shelled by enemy guns on a track taking us there, for which they obviously had the exact range. Arthur stopped the Jeep. He said later he had never seen anyone leap for cover as fast as I did. I decided that perhaps I had made the right decision to go home. Lord Moran, Churchill's doctor, wrote a book on courage, advancing a theory that most men have a stock of courage, which can be reduced, and ultimately exhausted.

The shelling stopped, we went on, and reached troop headquarters, functioning in an old Italian farmhouse. The family, including women, were still living there, even though it was periodically under fire: this was something new to me, who had been used to war in a vast empty desert. Indeed the Germans here were only just over the ridge, and were using a new weapon to me, a nine-barrelled mortar which made a weird moaning sound.

I then said a final goodbye and moved some 40 miles to where the 10th Hussars had left their rear wagon lines. There was a tent mess and one or two officers, including a Captain the Viscount Ednam, who was convalescing after being wounded in the Gothic line battle of the 4th September. I suppose this must have been towards the end of September, and I stayed a day or two before being conveyed to railhead for the 300 mile journey to Naples.

The train was of cattle trucks, the type that used to be labelled Quarante et Huit. These wagons of French origin were once designed to hold 40 men or eight horses, and were used also by the Germans during this war to transport troops, war prisoners, horses, freight, and civilian prisoners to concentration camps. But we were only about eight men to a truck, making it quite comfortable. We were given rations, three days per man which seemed generous for 300 miles. But we were to learn differently. We equipped ourselves with petrol cans cut in half and filled with earth, and brew cans and water so tea was assured. I had an enormous amount of kit, including a tin trunk, and a 17 pounder ammo box full of books, and a camp bed. Fortunately there was plenty of room in the truck for all this. I shared with seven assorted ordinary ranks. What route we followed I do not know, but the train started, travelled for 10 miles then stopped.

When it moved on again it might go for five minutes, it might go for a couple of hours. When it stopped we had no idea for how long – sometimes for three minutes, sometimes for three hours. At a stop we used to hop out and get a brew on, and sometimes without the slightest warning we would quickly hear a clank-clank-clank all along the train as the couplings tightened up and it moved off. We then had to douse the fire and sweep it up complete with brew can onto the floor of the cattle truck, running beside it the while, then jump back in.

On the fourth day our food was virtually gone. When we halted, one man went off to a farm we could see several hundred yards away, to get eggs. As he disappeared the train started and that was the last we saw of him.

1944 (OCTOBER)
CHAPTER 15

AMAZING ENCOUNTER
…BROTHER PETER, OUT OF NOWHERE

As the only officer in my part of the train I decided I must try to acquire some rations. At a long halt I somehow found out a building I could see some hundreds of yards away was a DID – an RASA ration depot. I had a word with the Italian engine driver, telling him I was going over there, as best I could, took two men and persuaded the D.I.D. to part with a day's rations for 30 men or whatever. While collecting them I was anxiously looking over my shoulder all the while, fearing the train would move off. I needn't have worried: it was there for hours after we got back.

The fifth day dawned and soon our rations were again exhausted. When we halted I asked a railwayman walking down the line how far from Naples we were and he said, to my delight, "30 kilometres." He then uncoupled us from the truck in front and walked away: why, I have no idea.

However, since the front of the train also contained men going to Naples I saw no reason why we should be separated from them, so I got on the line and coupled us on again. In a few minutes the train started again, and I must confess to some anxiety as to what the effect of my action might be until, within an hour, we were steaming into a station marked boldly Napoli.

I now found myself in a transit camp, sharing a tent with a couple of other chaps who constantly gave a spirited rendering of a song to be heard every night at the Orange Grove, the open air nightclub. It was, I found, called Come back to Sorrento, and it was, and is, a super song which soon everyone in England was humming. I had to wait for a ship home, which ultimately did not come for a month, and of course I was rather trapped because I had no transport of my own, something to which I was totally unaccustomed.

Fortunately I could sometimes borrow a truck and a passion wagon was laid on to the Orange Grove sometimes in the evenings, or to the officers club. I recall meeting there a remarkable man, a Lt Colonel* commanding a battalion of the Skins (The Royal Enniskillen Fusiliers). He had landed in Algeria with the 1st Army as a sergeant in November 1942: in April 1943 at Longstop Hill all his company officers were casualties and he was commissioned in the field, and now 18 months later he was commanding his battalion. His junior officers thought him a marvel, and indeed for a regular ranker it was the most rapid promotion I knew of.

*He was Lt. Col. TM Slane MC and was actually commissioned 1/1/41. He was promoted to command the Battalion in March 1944 at the age of 25 (Regimental History).

I persuaded a small group of others to join me in a visit to the San Carlo Opera, Italy's most famous after the Scala at Milan. They were doing Madame Butterfly, and we occupied one of the many boxes in the dress circles. The performance was preceded by the national anthems of France, the USA and our own. Until then I had always thought our own anthem rather uninspiring, but somehow after the other two it seemed to have a grandeur I had never realised. The singing was marvellous and the sets spectacular, with a moon in one act which slowly moved its position in the sky as time went by. Nevertheless, I was the only one that fell asleep.

I was detailed to join a court sitting permanently for court martials in Naples. I sat for three days and heard several cases. The first was a cook charged with selling rations and we had no difficulty in finding him guilty. I was sitting with a major and a captain, but I was asked first for the verdict, as the junior officer.

That was alright, but not so easy when it came to the sentence. The senior officer read out the range of penalties, which seemed to run from seven days confined to barracks to death. I suggested six months prison, and the two others said three months and 12 months respectively; we compromised on my figure of six months. It was a pretty bad case, for he had being doing it on a large scale.

Next day two of us sat with a member of the Judge Advocate General's department, with a professional lawyer as senior officer. The accused was a military police sergeant who had been caught in flagrante delicto, indulging with an Italian prostitute in various practices I shall not relate. He was supposed to be arresting her but apparently accepted her services instead. An Italian civilian man was a witness and was asked to describe exactly what happened: it so chanced that the Italian interpreter was a woman. Nothing could induce the witness to answer the questions of the president of the court martial, and it became obvious he was not going to describe the sexual events which had occurred to this interpreter, who might have had some difficulty in translating. With no other interpreter available, the case had to be adjourned until next day. Only then did we find out what had happened. The whole case was bizarre!

Shortly after we had left Algiers, Bill and Sheila also left to join Allied Headquarters at Caserta, 20 miles from Naples. This HQ was in the Royal Palace of the Kingdom of Naples, completed in 1774, a vast building of 1,200 rooms built around four courts. The wrennery was nearby and I was able to get over to see her, which was pleasant, and to arrange another visit in a few days. She had arrived in Naples just before the summer 1944 eruption of Vesuvius, a spectacular sight. By the time I arrived it had settled down to just a plume of smoke.

A day or two later I arrived at the wrennery again and started to walk along the side of the buildings, noting casually a naval officer,

As he reached me I stopped and stared. He stopped. And I gasped "Peter?" It was indeed my brother Peter, whom I had last seen as a boy of 16, and now miraculously stood before me as a young man of 21.

approaching me from the opposite direction in the distance. As he got nearer he looked somehow familiar, and I saw that he was not Navy but Merchant Navy, with a moustache. As he reached me I stopped and stared. He stopped. And I gasped "Peter?" It was

AMAZING ENCOUNTER ...BROTHER PETER, OUT OF NOWHERE

1944, brother Peter

indeed my brother Peter, whom I had last seen as a boy of 16, and now miraculously stood before me as a young man of 21.

I had no idea where in the world he had been of recent months: the last I had heard he was in South Africa, or the Far East, or Canada or somewhere and I was so amazed I could hardly speak for two minutes.

However, Peter filled the gap. He described how, knowing I had a girlfriend in Naples called Bill, he decided to visit her when his ship berthed at Torre Annunziata, a commercial port in Naples Bay. Using his initiative, he had made his way to the wrennery and asked for Bill, who reported I had been up in the line near Ancona, but was on my way back to Naples. He took her out once or twice and was able to plan a meeting when I arrived in Naples. I rang Bill to say I would come to see her next day.

We all went out together, hitch-hiking I suppose, and Peter's ship then sailed. It is remarkable that he happened to arrive at Naples for a few days just when I was there. Pete reminded me that we went out together in the evening to the officers club near the Castel Dell Ovo and drank Lachrima Christi out of glasses made from cut-off beer bottles.

I used to see Bill every few days when she was off duty, and one day I succeeded in obtaining a 15 cwt truck in which we went to Sorrento. It was a nightmare journey, quite far on roads covered in deep potholes, and the springing like iron. I always used to say the Ford 15 cwts really needed a three ton load to make them comfortable to ride. However, Sorrento itself was lovely. We lunched in the YWCA, which was on the cliff overlooking the

Bay of Naples. We also went to Pompeii.

At last I embarked upon the ship for home. There were six of us in two triple bunks in a small cabin, and the ship was dry. That didn't worry me, but it very much worried a certain officer who used to go about buttonholing people and begging them to sell him something to drink. He was obviously an alcoholic and I saw him being lowered over the side lashed to a stretcher as we lay off Gibraltar. Through the Straits we thought the journey would soon be over, but no. We went far out into the Atlantic to avoid submarines, and it was many days more before we found ourselves cruising slowly up a wide grey river lined with dingy buildings dimly discernible through the November mist. It was the Mersey, and soon I could discern the outline of the Liver building on the left.

If I had only known it, Beryl Lefroy was probably involved in directing the movement of our convoy from the Atlantic into the Mersey. Before disembarking I arranged with Wardley, a shipboard friend, to meet him in London later for a few days: he said airily that his father would arrange a hotel – which indeed he did.

Two or three times on board an announcement had come over the Tannoy stating all illegally held arms should be handed in, which I had ignored. I had taken the precaution of packing my Luger in the middle of my tin trunk, confident no-one would have time to examine luggage on landing. This proved to be the case, and somehow I managed to collect together my huge pile of kit and move it to the adjoining station. At 7pm that night I reached Midland Station Nottingham to begin my month's disembarkation leave.

With a porter's help I got my kit as far as the entrance hall, only to find a long queue for the few taxis. It was time for a little initiative so I struck a bargain with an Evening News van waiting there, loaded everything in the back, and in 10 minutes was drawing up at 64 Burlington Road. I could imagine for myself later how it felt for my mother and father to see me again after five years. They both looked older and slower, as indeed they were, and I felt the war had taken its toll on them with years of hard work and worry, and both sons continually absent abroad.

It was good to be home, but leave was a disappointment. None of my friends was about, indeed nobody I knew at all. Of school friends to whom I had been close, Derek Hayes and David Banwell were in India. Geoffrey Whiteley had seriously broken his leg dropping in France by parachute on D-Day, and was convalescing somewhere. Roger and Lionel West were both, by an odd coincidence, drowned. Roger, Derek and I

I could imagine for myself later how it felt for my mother and father to see me again after five years. They both looked older and slower, as indeed they were, and I felt the war had taken its toll on them with years of hard work and worry, and both sons continually absent abroad.

had formed the whole of the photographic society at the Nottingham high school before the war. Roger had gone to Cambridge, rowed for his college and, on graduating had joined the Indian Civil Service. He had been drowned trying to cross a flooded river to take supplies to the Indians, for whom he was a district officer.

Lionel, his younger brother, was among the glider troops in 1st Airborne Division who were dropped in the sea off Sicily at the time of the invasion, when the American pilot of the towing aircraft didn't like the flak he was getting. I always felt very sorry for Mrs West, particularly when the rest of us turned up safe and sound after the war.

1944-45 (NOVEMBER-APRIL)
CHAPTER 16

STAGE DOOR JOHNNY
...FOR GOSSIP, NOT THE GIRL

To revert to my leave, the first thing to do was to buy a car, and my godfather Arthur Dickins put me on to a little man who produced a 1937 Morris 8, which I bought for £100. I sold it six years later for £250. Soldiers on leave from abroad had a small petrol ration, so I collected my coupons. I took the train to London to meet Wardley. His father was the managing director of Thomas de la Rue, printer of all the country's banknotes, and he had paid for a suite at the Russell Hotel in Bloomsbury where his son and I lived in style for several days. I cannot say the visit was a tremendous success, because it turned out that Wardley and I had not a great deal in common.

However, I recall that the first night he took us to dinner at the Cafe Royal. In those days there was a maximum spend of five shillings on any meal, but luxury establishments could add a house charge. The Savoy house charge was, I think, seven shillings and six pence, and the Cafe Royal was probably five shillings, but it was certainly a rather super place. I recall we had game pie, to me a fabulous luxury compared with the food I had lived on for years, but Mr Wardley leaned over anxiously to ask "I hope you found it eatable?" I gravely assured him that I did, but the expression became one used in our family for years.

We went out to one or two night clubs; Murrays and the Astor, I remember, with a couple of Sloanes whom Wardley knew, and who were from the Princess Royal's Volunteer Corps, I think, a socially acceptable service, but with whom I did not empathize. Rather better was Bunty, Wardley's sister. She was in a ballet at The Hippodrome. It was not so much the girl herself who was the attraction as the business of going in the stage door to wait for her after the show, and gossiping with the stage doorkeeper.

My leave over, I reported back to the Royal Artillery's base depot at Woolwich to await a posting. One attended a morning parade and the authorities were only too glad not to have to find anything for one to do. I therefore quickly learned that the best procedure was to step quickly forward and ask permission to be released to see one's banker, tailor or

The buzz bombs had stopped but London was still getting the V2 rockets. These were only apparent from the occasional sound of an explosion near or far: I was never close to one.

anything else one could think of. I was thereby enabled to see the main London sights. The buzz bombs had stopped but London was still getting the V2 rockets. These were only apparent from the occasional sound of an explosion near or far: I was never close to one. I attended a field gunnery course at Larkhill on Salisbury Plain, of which all I recall is being on an exercise early one morning and seeing Stonehenge loom out of the mist right in front of me. There were no fences round it in those days, and seen through the mist, empty of people, it was strangely impressive.

There was plenty of social life in the evenings in London in those days, although one had to leave fairly early to catch the Tube. There was, for instance, a rather select club for officers in Knightsbridge run by Sloane Rangers with whom one danced and socialised. Hospitals used to run dances attended by nurses and medical students, and at the Royal Free I met a medical student called Pauline whom I took out a few times. I stayed one weekend at her family home in Rochester, where her father was the gas manager. It sounds rather like something out of Beachcomber. Rochester gas manager – indeed Rochester itself on a damp January Saturday was not pulsating. I cannot recall doing any work while I was at Woolwich, apart from being in charge for a day or two of an officer locked up under close arrest.

I was soon posted to the 6th Regiment, Royal Horse Artillery, a very superior regiment, and found myself in Rocket Troop. We were at Shoreham and officers of Rocket Troop (really a battery, not a troop) were billeted at the house of AA Milne, author of Winnie the Pooh and Christopher Robin books. We were equipped with SP 25 pounders (self-propelled field guns) which to the uninitiated looked very like tanks. We used to train on the South Downs and come March it was so sunny that on maintenance sessions the troops were in shirt sleeve order. I quickly learned to handle a tank and used to take a tank full of trainee drivers into Brighton for driving practice. A tank being moved any distance, however, was taken on a transporter: driving it up two ramps was not easy, but backing it off was distinctly hairy.

On a Sunday several of us would go on a long walk over the downs to Chanctonbury Ring, a prehistoric hill fort atop Chanctonbury Hill which became a site of Special Scientific Interest on the South Downs. We then had tea at Steyning, one of the prettiest of Sussex towns. On Saturdays we would drive over to Brighton, where we patronised the bar at the Dome dance hall. But this was England, and petrol and transport were much more difficult to get here than abroad.

However, the war in Europe was obviously nearing its end, and there was generally a light-hearted feeling about. But suddenly the regiment was told it would sail for the Far East in a fortnight. I had already been overseas for five years and the policy was not to send such men to the Far East. So after only six weeks with the Royal Horse Artillery I was back to Woolwich again.

I was only there long enough to meet Peter, who by then was in the port of London. Somehow he contacted me and we arranged to meet outside a theatre where Vivien Leigh was playing in The Skin of our Teeth, the intellectual hit of the day. I waited till last minute, but Peter was late, so I left his ticket at the box office and went in and took my seat. The curtain had just risen when Peter slipped into the seat beside me.

Early in April I crossed the Channel and arrived at a transit camp in Belgium to await a posting. It was in a convent at Contick, about six miles outside Antwerp and, oddly enough, nuns still occupied half of it. When I used to meet one of the nuns walking in the gardens we would bow and smile politely at one another. However, I was billeted on an old

English lady who had been married to a Belgian and had lived in Belgium for 50 years. In consequence her English was both rusty and accented, and we often used to speak in French, since my French was fairly good after using it a lot in Egypt and Algeria.

I was the only soldier in her large house and she had a real library, one room with four walls lined from floor to ceiling with books, many in English. Being called on to do no duties, I was there a month, and I read solidly, usually sitting out in the large garden. She had standard works there I would otherwise never have seen, such as Lecky's History of European Morals, Malthus, Gibbon and so on, and I think I improved my education. The old lady had no flour, and used to make a substitute by pounding potatoes in water and sieving the result finely. It was extremely laborious and brought home to me the fact Europeans had suffered food shortages a lot more than we had in the UK.

Occasionally I went into Antwerp, where there seemed little to see. However, there was a fast electric train to Brussels, a mere 30 miles, which enabled me to see something of the capital, although I saw a lot more later on leave from Germany. I admired the Grande Place, and entered what I thought was a very attractive cafe on one corner: it turned out to be a private club, but they made me welcome. I somehow knew a Belgian civilian and one day joined a group of about 10 young people at an Antwerp cafe table. I was, of course, introduced to and shook hands with them all. The group's composition was constantly changing, and every time someone joined it was handshakes all round: every time someone left, the same. After about half an hour of this I was glad to escape.

1945 (MAY-NOVEMBER)
CHAPTER 17
A NATIONAL DILEMMA
TO FRATERNISE OR NOT?

A NATIONAL DILEMMA TO FRATERNISE OR NOT?

On 7th May, VE Day, I arrived at Hamburg and joined 323 Battery in the 81st Field Regiment. I arrived late. Everyone was out somewhere. All I could do was go to bed, so I never celebrated VE Day. Next day I learned tragedy had taken place the night before in the sergeants' mess. Two sergeants, close friends, had a William Tell party trick with one raising a rifle and the other standing with a cigarette tin on top of his head. This time it had gone wrong; one shot the other through the head, stone dead.

I was soon made welcome but quickly found there was no work for me. The men were all detached on various guard duties and the only work for any officers was administrative. So few people except the battery commander and battery captain had much to do at all. At least we would enjoy the fruits of victory. The house of Herr Reenitsa, a tobacco millionaire, was commandeered as an officers' club: it was a magnificent modern mansion, Hollywood style. It had a large library, mostly of books in German, but I discovered a beautifully bound and illustrated copy of A Midsummer Night's Dream in English which I removed, thinking Herr Reenitsa would have no further use for it.

One Sunday night there was a concert in the Hamburg Opera House: it was only about an hour long, which suited most of us non-musical English admirably, and they played popular classics, like Eine Kleine Nachtmusik. I first heard there a duet, Meine Liebe, Deine Liebe, something charming by Oscar Strauss: I am surprised I never heard it in England.

Although I bought a good leather bag for occupation marks, cigarettes became the real currency. Every week I gave my batman a packet of 10 cigarettes to sell for me from my free issue of 50: proceeds paid my mess bills, and I continued this procedure the whole time I was there.

The battery commander organised a German teacher to come and give us lessons, which at least started me off in the language. I had previously done two terms of German in the science sixth at school, but did not remember much of it. Even these lessons did not achieve much, since we only stayed in Hamburg for three weeks. Our teacher was a nice man, in a much darned suit. I realised here something of what the war had cost the Germans.

Firstly there were miles of ruined or flattened buildings, and what happened in Hamburg was repeated everywhere. There were few men between 18 and 50, and it was remarkable how many of those were devoid of a leg or an arm. There had been a great shortage of military doctors, and in innumerable cases a wounded limb was just chopped off, partly because of shortage of

I realised here something of what the war had cost the Germans. Firstly there were miles of ruined or flattened buildings, and what happened in Hamburg was repeated everywhere. There were few men between 18 and 50, and it was remarkable how many of those were devoid of a leg or an arm.

1945, Hamburg, July

hospitals and of time, and partly because they used medics with only 18 months' training. When driving through a town there seemed to be no shops visible, since all the windows were broken or were boarded up, with no lights and nothing in them anyway.

I had the address of the German sergeant major who was one of my captors in Tunis in 1945, and with whom I had made a bet as to who would win the war. I expected he was dead, if not he was in a POW camp, but the district where he had lived was absolutely flat. Etched on my mind is the picture of a trapdoor in the ground opening, obviously the entrance to a cellar, from which emerged a girl in a fresh white dress. What morale, I thought, to live in a cellar yet keep oneself so smart. From what I learned later of conditions generally, that was probably the only dress she had.

The only work I had to do in the three weeks we remained at Hamburg was to take charge of an opencast brown coal mine and the attached factory which made the stuff into briquettes. I inspected it all with the manager, but hadn't the foggiest idea what else I was supposed to do. I indicated we should be watching his production carefully and left. Fortunately, the Control Commission soon took over.

The unit then moved down to the Ruhr area and my battery were in a modest country house at Juchen, some 15 miles west of Dusseldorf. Here I got my first opportunity to ride. I learned of a girl described as a vet, who had horses, and I called on her. She was only about 20, and must really have been a veterinary assistant, but sure enough she had a horse in the back garden of the semi-detached house where she lodged, and access to other horses. I arranged to call again next day for a ride and, sure enough, she had a horse for me which I mounted and for the first day I felt myself shaken about like a sack of coals. She laughed incessantly but I didn't fall off, and after a few days of riding every day I could get along quite nicely.

We rode together every day and I graduated to riding bareback (extremely uncomfortable) and to riding down steep slopes, Western style. One day she provided a thoroughbred ("ein vollblut") and we had a tremendous race, which I won because I had much the best horse. I loved galloping, but having no great attachment to horses I found it very satisfactory to hand over the horse at the end of the ride to be groomed by somebody else. I paid nothing for all this, except maybe a few cigarettes. I also rode the regimental horses.

The pattern was to ride in the morning, sleep in the afternoon and party at night, but this happy state of affairs was interrupted after about a month by an attachment, with a party of drivers, to a small unit at Mulheim. It seemed it was a group collected from different sources, and the mess of about six officers was headed by a major in the Hampshires who held the VC, the only one I have ever known personally. The mess occupied the house of Hugo Stinnes, a former German steel magnate second only to Krupp. There was a vast air-raid shelter in the garden about 60 feet below ground.

I slept in a nice modern house opposite which had a grand piano and some music, and I spent many hours practising and trying to revive the very modest playing level I had reached as a boy. Here I first discovered, and frequently played, Beethoven's very easy Fur Elise. Here too I acquired a girlfriend by the name of Doris: she was a Sudeten German, but came from what she called the Protectorate, i.e. Czechoslovakia. Although only 19 she was the widow of a German officer: Germany was full of widows then. In view of the non-fraternization rules it was useful that she was Czech. From the start the Army had instituted a law of virtual apartheid: there must be no fraternization between allied troops and Germans – men or women – other than anything that might be required by one's duties.

This asked too much of human nature. Nevertheless some commanders enforced it and the military police did, although there was a good deal of turning a blind eye. Personally, I found I liked and could get on with Germans of both sexes: I felt much more at home with them than with the Latin races. That surprised me considerably having had them as enemies for nearly six years.

It rained continuously throughout August: at the time it seemed a worse month for weather than I had ever encountered in England. I moved again with my drivers, this time to a unit of the Royal Army Service Corps, whom I found most depressing – dreadful people. On return to the 81st Field, I was informed I was now eligible for LILOP - Leave In Lieu of Python, Python being the code name for the scheme whereby one was posted back to the UK after five years abroad (the Army loved acronyms and code names.)

I pointed out that I had already enjoyed the benefit of Python and could therefore

Personally, I found I liked and could get on with Germans of both sexes: I felt much more at home with them than with the Latin races. That surprised me considerably having had them as enemies for nearly six years.

> **I got into the Strangers' Gallery, which was in the House of Lords (the Commons having been bombed) in time to see Churchill rise to speak. The House was full to hear the prime minister although his subject, Poland, was dull. Nevertheless I was very glad to see and hear the great man in action.**

hardly have LILOP as well, but it was no use; on one month's leave to the UK I had to go. However, I made good use of it. I paid a short visit to London and, having previously made arrangements with my MP, went to the Houses of Parliament. I jumped into a taxi outside the officers' club where I was staying and said smartly "House of Commons!" "Members entrance?" asked the driver – I was wearing service dress and I might, of course, have been a member.

I got into the Strangers' Gallery, which was in the House of Lords (the Commons having been bombed) in time to see Churchill rise to speak. The House was full to hear the prime minister although his subject, Poland, was dull. Nevertheless I was very glad to see and hear the great man in action. I also met Bill for lunch, our rendezvous being outside Swan & Edgar's – where else? Everybody always met outside Swan & Edgar's in Piccadilly Circus. As we were strolling up Whitehall afterwards, the Mounted Life Guard on sentry duty outside the Horse Guards came smartly to the salute with his sword, the only time I have ever been saluted with a sword.

I also went up to the Lake District for a few days walking, perforce alone. I stayed at the Lodore Hotel in Borrowdale, having gone by train to Keswick then by taxi: not enough petrol coupons to go in my car bought a year before. The hotel was full of old ladies living there permanently, who each had their own labelled pot of jam or marmalade on their own table.

It was the end of November and snowed heavily, and I recall ploughing along the top of the ridge from Cat Bells over Maiden Moor in deep snow and mist.

A NATIONAL DILEMMA TO FRATERNISE OR NOT?

1945 (WINTER)
CHAPTER 18
AMONG THE ARISTOCRACY
...SURVIVORS OF CONFLICT

Back with the regiment in Germany, I also somehow contrived three days' leave in Brussels, where I met Nick Smith whom I had not seen since 1943. We visited the Musée Royal, particularly to see a number of Brueghels, and also the Wiertz Museum which my father had visited pre-1914. We than had an extended night out, chiefly in one little club where I kept on tipping the musicians every half hour so that they would keep going.

We left at 5am and drove around the empty Brussels streets in Nick's Jeep until we found ourselves outside the Palais de Justice, a gigantic building reputedly the largest erected in the 19th Century. In front are steps, with colonnades along the sides – we drove up the steps and along the colonnade at one side until we could go no further; it was fascinating how well the Jeep managed quite steep steps.

It was now nearly Christmas, and someone had the bright idea of inviting some girls as our guests from the neighbouring camp of South American Displaced Persons. We had visions of glamorous Argentinian senoritas, but when they turned up to join us for Christmas dinner in the evening they proved to be as unattractive as could be imagined.

However, we entertained them as politely as we could and then – just as they were about to leave – Douglas, who by then was drunk and ridiculously cheerful, invited them all again for Boxing Day, which was promptly accepted. Next morning, he agreed he must have been mad, but at the close of the Boxing Night party, sure enough, he invited them again and would accept no denials from the rest of us. This time we sent a message the following morning to the camp leader to say that we regretted it would not be convenient for us to receive his inmates that night, and that was the last we saw of them.

There were at this time vast numbers of displaced persons still in Germany who had been imported as slave labour. Nationalities such as the French were quickly repatriated but others took longer, particularly Russians. The Russian peasant women were huge: the men used to indulge in quite a lot of rape of German women, no doubt partly as revenge, but it caused a political problem for the Allied Control Commission, and local Germans sometimes came and complained to us.

But now came one of the most pleasant periods of my whole war. Dai Gilbertson was a battery commander in 324 Battery of 81st Field Artillery, an extrovert with a face like an elf, and pointed ears. He decided to form a ski club for use by all ranks of the Artillery Brigade of the 53rd Welsh Division, which included us (since my commission I had spent half my time in a South Wales unit, i.e. the 81st Field). He reconnoitred carefully the area of the Hoch Sauerland, about 130 miles from our regional headquarters at Greuenbroich in the Rhineland. Although not high, the mountains being under 3,000 feet, it was very popular with Germans from the Ruhr because it was so near, although now, of course, they had no means of travelling.

The place he picked upon was the Gasthof Rossel at Neuastenberg, about three miles from the main village resort of Winterberg.

Above left: 1945, Brussels, Joyce Carr. Above right: 1945, Brussels, DGM. Below: 1945, Brussels, The Royal Palace

AMONG THE ARISTOCRACY ...SURVIVORS OF CONFLICT

1945, Brussels

Dai asked my battery to provide what was, in effect, someone for the hotel manager's job, and I was lucky enough to be picked. He also found from somewhere a major by the name of Robbie Mills, an experienced skier who had been a member of the Downhill Only Club at Wengen before the war, and who was to act as ski instructor.

Immediately after Christmas, Dai and I drove to the club and I was introduced to Herr and Frau Rossel. Dai then went back to the regiment and I was left for a week, the lone Englishman in this German mountain village, to organise ready for the first guests early in the New Year. Having arranged with the nearest DID to draw rations on the basis of our number of visitors, and having had Robbie arrive with supplies of skis and boots, there was not much else to do, and I made contact with a party of young Germans who were staying at the inn opposite.

I suppose they were aged about 20 to 21: how they had escaped the forces I do not know, but probably the young men were at university. As for the girls, certainly Erika, nicknamed Ei, worked in a bank, and we quickly struck up a friendship. I spent all my time with these young Germans for a week: although I could not ski I quickly picked up enough to join in the langlauf, and we'd ski over miles of forest trails. After the evening meal I would go over and join them in drinking some appalling beer which was all that was then available. We wanted to sing: there was a piano, and sheet music, but amazingly none of these Germans could play, so I set to and did the best I could.

Early in January our first guests arrived, also Dai and Robbie. There was Kurt too, the 17-year-old son of the proprietor of the Dusseldorf sports shop supplying the skis and boots. While I never concerned myself with financial aspects of dealing with the Germans, I imagine we housed and fed him for three months in return for his father supplying us with skis and boots. Robbie had also brought his girlfriend, Margot Plucker, nominally as club secretary, and she was, I must say, very attractive. By this time my German was pretty good for conversation purposes and since I learned it like a child, by talking with others, I believe my accent was quite reasonable.

We engaged two expert local Germans as ski instructors, Heinrich Pape and a chap called Hans. While Hans was really a local peasant, Heinrich was a good looking, intelligent and well spoken man in his 30s who had been in the 1936 Olympic team. The club was an all ranks one, some of the officers had skied before, but none of the others, and it was the job of Hans and Heinrich to get them ski-ing in the week they usually spent with us.

This was not so easy as it would be now, because there was no ski lift or ski tow, so one spent hours laboriously walking up the slope, and runs tended to be short. There was also no piste as such, although obviously one tended to be created in certain places. We experimented with an old RAF winch which we got hold of, and used it as a ski tow, but it kept on breaking down and was not a success. The whole thing would have been terrible by modern standards, but almost everyone enjoyed it all immensely. I could usually only find time to ski in the afternoons, but in due course I was doing parallel turns.

Mornings were usually occupied. I had to collect rations and agree the menu with Frau Rossel. She was a good cook and we had superb meals, including a particularly delicious chocolate pudding. I acquired the wine and we had quite a good cellar including Sekt, the German champagne, of which we drank a vast quantity. I recall going on a wine buying expedition with Dai Gilbertson down the Rhine. I allocated the rooms to guests and was responsible for the mess bills: I suppose we had about 10 or 12 rooms and fortunately the inn had wood-fired central heating.

From an early date it was understood that regular visitors could bring their girl friends, if we had room. Margot Plucker, as club secretary, was a permanent resident. Dai Gilbertson came with Elise, the daughter of a wealthy Dusseldorf factory owner, and Mike Dowding with Ursula, Baroness von Ziegesen. A Polish cavalry officer, Captain Franowski, brought the Countess von Kalnein. All this departed considerably from the original concept of an artillery club, but it quickly became apparent that there was not sufficient demand from the artillery only, and it was certainly much more fun this way.

Apres ski was excellent, with hot gluhwein always ready at about 4pm and a party with unlimited Sekt every evening. Our favourite after dinner game was played standing on a marked line with an empty champagne bottle in each hand. (They had to be champagne bottles to be strong enough.) One bent forward as far as one could, and supporting oneself on one bottle, reached forward with the other hand and stood it upright as far forward as possible. With practice, it was surprising how far one could reach, and Robbie and I, being resident, took a lot of beating.

We had other entertainment besides our local ski-ing. Sometimes a race was organised in conjunction with another British ski club in Winterberg, the bigger village three miles away. From time to time the taciturn Herr Rossel would get out his horse sledge and one could have the pleasure of riding in it, or being towed on skis behind, called ski-joring. Better, and faster, was ski-joring along the road behind a car. Most exciting to watch, however, were the ski jumping competitions held by the locals on Sundays. The ski jump was not very high compared with the international jumping one saw on television later, but it was the most exciting sport I have ever watched. I only ever saw one Englishman do it, a young soldier: he wasn't very good, didn't jump very far, and usually fell on landing, but he was terribly brave.

If one looks down the jump from the top, as I have done, it is a terrifying spectacle: one cannot see the landing slope below, and it looks as if you are jumping into space. I used to stand on the side of the slope just below the jump and as the skier flew through the air past me his clothes, which were loose, made a rapid cracking sound like sails in a gale, adding somehow to the excitement. The young men of the village, of course, started to learn as children – they were on little skis at five – and took to ski jumping like young Englishmen might to rugby. They could usually jump up to 50 metres, and although I saw many terrible falls I never saw anyone hurt. Fired by this, I experimented by making a little step in the snow about a foot high. Even with this, one could jump several metres, but it was very difficult to land without falling.

Sometimes I would have to go back to the Battery, perhaps to collect wine, and on one occasion coming back to Neuastenberg as a passenger in the front seat of a truck, the offside front wheel came off. First we knew of it was the sight of a wheel bowling along the road in front of us, and I had just time to say "I wonder where that has come from" when the truck tipped down on its front axle and we scraped to a halt. Something had sheared, there was no repairing it, and it was nearly dark. There was nothing for my driver and me but to walk to the nearest cottage and demand a bed. We got it, but no food, and no heating, and it was perishing cold, until we were able to make contact with help next day.

I thought some venison would add to our already admirable diet, so I paid a visit to the adjoining largest landowner in her schloss, the Princess von Wittgeustein. I was shown into a large drawing room containing an occasional table on which the Almanack de

Gotha (the German Debrett) lay conspicuously open. The middle-aged princess was very pleasant and readily said she would instruct her keeper to shoot a deer for us, which he did. We had some excellent venison cooked in various ways for some time.

Despite Germany having been a republic since 1918, the old aristocracy seemed to have survived very well. At Winterberg the next village Wilhelm, former Crown Prince of Prussia, was ski-ing. One of our guests at the club had met him there and insisted on referring to him, no doubt correctly, as Willy

He then casually mentioned he thought we would all go over his point to point course! I had never taken a jump in my life but I had no option but to reply, equally casually, that it seemed a good idea.

Prussia... Countess Inge von Kalnein, who came to the club with the Baroness Gisela, friend of Mike Dowding, temporarily fell out with her Polish captain and invited me down to the family home, Lauvenburg, near the Rhine for the weekend. It was a most interesting experience to see German life from the inside.

Lauvenburg was a large country house, the home I think of her uncle: Inge and her younger sister had fled the family estates in East Germany ahead of the advancing Russians. She once asked me how old I thought she was: I thought she looked about the same as I, 26 or 27. I suggested tactfully she might be 22. She was 18! We normally spoke German together although the uncle spoke excellent English. I visited Lauvenburg again later and stayed overnight when they held a big dance, and I was impressed by how they had managed to get together such generous food and drink and warmth. On my first, more private visit, the family were living in one small room for warmth and eating pretty sparsely, and of very poor quality.

On one of these two visits I was invited by our Polish captain to the Cavalry Remount Depot near Lauvenburg, which he commanded. I was glad to accept and fortunately I had a good pair of leather riding boots which I had bought from a fellow officer, and the breeches which I had made in Lincoln in December 1939! I inspected the stables and the horses were all in beautiful condition. He and I then went out into the yard and the men, each standing by his horse, were drawn up in line and called to attention. He saluted me and invited me to mount and lead off, which I did with him alongside. He then casually mentioned he thought we would all go over his point to point course! I had never taken a jump in my life but I had no option but to reply, equally casually, that it seemed a good idea.

We arrived at the first jump, which seemed extremely high, and of course I was invited to take the damn thing first. I cantered up to it, but the horse knew very well I didn't know what I was doing, and refused. After two refusals, the captain suggested my mount would probably go with the others if we all went over. Indeed this was so, and we sailed high in the air, and I lost my left stirrup. I stayed on though, and for the next hundred yards fought hard to get my foot back in, which I did just in time for the next fence. This seemed lower and we sailed over without difficulty, and I thoroughly enjoyed the rest of the course.

I am quite sure that the captain (I cannot remember his Christian name and his surname is ridiculous) was trying to take the mickey out of me, and although he succeeded to a certain extent, I did not completely disgrace myself, since I did take all the fences and I didn't fall off. It was certainly an experience that got the adrenalin going.

Back at the ski club Robbie Mills left in February, being somewhat older and in an earlier demob group. I was in group 25, which had demobilisation deferred for three months. It is laughable, but typically army, that most of those three months I spent running the ski club. The last guest left 13th March, and I stayed on for a few days to close things down.

Before I left, I toured the Hochsaverland, where they had a speciality of wood-turning, and bought a number of wooden bowls, coasters, breadboards and a set of dolls' furniture, made in local country style. I thought I would save it for my daughters, but not having had any I saved for a grand-daughter. I bade farewell to the Rossel family and Toni, Herr Rossel's sister was quite emotional.

She was a kindly, sentimental spinster of perhaps 45 who, I was privately informed, used to console the village priest. When I expressed surprise, my informant said Toni's indignant comment was: "Well, he's a man, isn't he?"

After Robbie's departure I had become much epris with Margot, and when I got back to the battery I had only three weeks before demob. I used to go over to Wuppertal quite a lot to the family apartment to take her out, and I remember how pleasant the Ruhr Valley was in its super country reaches. Wuppertal was at that time chiefly distinguished by its oberbahn, an overhead railway which cunningly utilised space over the little river Wupper by faithfully following every curve of the river, supported on gantries with a foot on each bank. It ran for several miles as a local commuter train, and the coaches being below the single supporting rail.

1946 (MARCH-AUGUST)
CHAPTER 19

SINKING LOVE
HOW THE SEA COOLS PASSIONS

At times I drove through Essen, a vast heap of rubble that we were told would take 10 years to clear and 40 to rebuild. I believed it. In Cologne, the ancient cathedral stood, isolated but complete, amid a waste of bomb damage. The autobahns were still good for brief distances, but every one of the many bridges had been blown. Wherever a ruin of one remained one had to drive down a bumpy earth track, cross the minor road below, and up the other side. It was now almost a year since Germany's surrender, yet rebuilding had barely started, since I cannot recall seeing any at all.

In early April I left the regiment for the last time, travelled to Calais with all my kit including skis, across the Channel and on to demob at York. My release certificate showed 124 days leave starting 4th April 1946. I collected my demob suit, and as soon as I got back to Nottingham I took it to a little man whom Horace Claydon was able to recommend to me, up a little alleyway in Lace Market. I found him in a tiny room, surrounded by garments being altered, and sitting cross-legged on a table in the ancient and traditional way. He turned it into a respectable suit for me. I spent only a few days at home, and was in touch by letter with Nick Smith, who told me he was living in an old farmhouse up in the Pennines and invited me up for an indefinite period.

I drove up in Dulcie, the little 1937 Morris I had bought 18 months earlier. I wove my way laboriously up through Huddersfield, Halifax and Hebden Bridge, then out of the valley through the village of Heptonstall and on to a dirt road for a mile between stonewalled fields, until I stopped above Lower Fold. It was a traditional old English longhouse, probably 17th Century, with the barn at one end and the farmhouse at the other, although in this case there was also an empty cottage on the end of the house.

Inside was quite a large room and a living kitchen with an old fashioned coal range. Stone flagged floors, no gas or electricity of course, no drainage and only a single cold tap into a stone sink in the lean-to scullery. It was fed by a spring never known to have dried up, so at least he had cold running water. Nick rented it from Fred Feather, the adjoining small farmer, for the princely sum

At times I drove through Essen, a vast heap of rubble that we were told would take 10 years to clear and 40 to rebuild. I believed it.

of 3 shillings and 6 pence a week, or more than £17 perhaps now. Even then, and for such basic accommodation, it seemed a good bargain for the use of a house, barn and cottage.

With his demob gratuity, Nick had bought a 15 cwt ex-Army Ford truck, with which he was doing work for local farmers, and his principle was to work just enough to earn sufficient to live on, which then meant two days a week. A few weeks later, when Kay came to live with him, he used to give her two pounds a week housekeeping money and that was it. However, Nick and I were there alone in those evenings and would sit talking

Above left: 1946, Yorkshire Lower Fold, DGM
Left: 1946, Yorkshire Lower Fold, Nick Smith and Dick Hockin
Above: 1946, Yorkshire, Nick Smith, an early caving expert

SINKING LOVE HOW THE SEA COOLS PASSIONS

Above: 1946, Yorkshire, Nick Smith and Dick Hockin
Below: 1946, Widdop Reservoir, DGM

Above: 1946, Yorkshire, Widdop Crag, DGM
Below: 1946, Nick Smith

in front of the fire, in two rocking chairs he had bought for ten shillings each. The sole lighting was the dim flame of a hurricane lamp, and in many ways I felt life had not changed in the 300 years or so since the house was built.

Nell, the sheepdog, lay on the hearth, and sometimes I would play our only two records on the old wind-up gramophone. Even now, if I hear Chopin's Fantaisie Impromptu, or Marlene Dietrich singing 'See What the Boys in the Back Room Will Have,' it takes me back at once to those early days at Lower Fold. During the day we wandered fields and moors round about. There was only one inhabited group of cottages higher up the valley, and nearest neighbours were quarter of a mile away. There were other farmhouses, sometimes derelict, higher up the valley still, but they had become deserted because there was no road, and life was too hard in that inhospitable landscape.

A rough track led on to Widdop Reservoir, above which was Widdop Crag on which we once tackled one or two easy climbs. (I came to Lower Fold many times between 1946 and 1949, and the experiences are all merged together, so some things I recount may have happened on a later visit). Near the crag, for example, was an old empty, windowless, square farmhouse, deserted for years but still sound. Over the door the lintel bore the carved words "Dry Summer, 1692." It was evocative of long ago.

To me, Nick was the original hippie. He had opted out of ordinary life, but with the big difference that he supported himself rather than depending upon social security.

He lived a contented life, stripped down to the basic elements, and would work just enough to live on. In the few months since his demob he had grown a full dark beard (unknown then) and wore clogs, which he regarded as ideal footwear. I had always thought of clogs as rather like French sabots: they are not. They are leather boots with wooden soles and a good clog maker asks his customer to walk up and down the street outside to assess his gait, then shapes the clog soles accordingly.

I went home for a short time then returned. I had really only just started my four months' paid leave. By this time Nick had sent for Kay, whom he had known at university. He had only to send a message and she came: she never left. Nick must have been hell to live with, obstinate and ruthless, although many people found him fascinating company. Kay Mordell was an intelligent and pleasant girl, whose father had held the chair of pure mathematics at Cambridge. Reputedly, only half a dozen people in the world knew what he was talking about. Forty years afterwards, oddly enough, I heard his name again. The niece of my brother Peter's wife, Megan, who he married after the war, is married to a brilliant Turkish University lecturer in mathematics who said to Peter, "Ah, Mordell's Conjecture – a well known theory published years ago, which has only just been proved, by a German."

Nick and I worked for three days for his landlord, Fred Feather, muck spreading. Fred was a harassed and disorganised little man, and because this much should have been spread long before, it had become very hard and impacted. Nick shovelled the muck and I spread it with a fork: at the end of the first day I was so stiff I could hardly move: after two days I was better, and after three days I was OK.

The nearest pub was the oddly named New Delight in Jack Bridge, known as Newdy. It was kept by Elsie Whittaker who was once asked by a local farmer to go upstairs to bed with him. Elsie reported that as an added inducement he said: "Come on, Elsie, it'll nobbut tak two minutes!"

Elsie had a very happy relationship with the local police in Hebden Bridge. We once walked down the one and a half miles over field paths and entered the pub's side door to find a group of locals drinking pints in the kitchen. We arrived about 11pm. At midnight in walked the police sergeant and said to Elsie "Ee, I 'ad a rare job closing them down in t'Brig tonight: ay I'll 'ave a pint, thank you."

For some reason we had a papal dispensation, and opening hours meant nothing. We once spent all night there and went home to breakfast at 6am with a local farmer. His wife happily produced breakfast and expressed no surprise whatever. More surprisingly, the first course of the meal consisted of a cereal bowl filled with half a jar of marmalade and covered in cream. It felt rather like being faced with sheep's eyes, but the only thing to do was eat it.

As I have said, I was very much taken with Margot in Germany and still was. Talking it over with Nick, he said: "Why not fetch her?" At first it seemed impossible: because of the non-fraternization regulations I could not legally see her, let alone bring her out of Germany – an enemy alien. However, we decided it could be done, James Bond fashion, and we started to play what we called Exercise Margot.

We would cross the Channel in a small boat to Calais, leave it in the harbour, hitch-hike to Wuppertal in Germany, dress Margot in an ATS uniform, then with forged passes travel by train back to Calais. To avoid awkward queries at that point we would jump off the train as it slowed (as I knew it did) before Calais station. Then back to the boat and return to Dover, where we were confident a small boat coming in would not arouse suspicion. Margot would be without a ration book or identity card, true, but in the country one could survive without. Margot and I could initially live in the cottage forming the end of Nick's house, and I cleaned it out and painted the front door in anticipation.

First, we had to acquire a boat. Kay knew

As I have said, I was very much taken with Margot in Germany and still was. Talking it over with Nick, he said: "Why not fetch her?" At first it seemed impossible: because of the non-fraternization regulations I could not legally see her, let alone bring her out of Germany – an enemy alien. However, we decided it could be done, James Bond fashion, and we started to play what we called Exercise Margot.

somebody in South Wales with a yacht they were trying to sell, but it turned out he wanted £600, a prodigious sum. We decided to go down to Kent and see what we could pick up.

Kay borrowed an ATS uniform from a friend and I forged Army passes with a child's printing set – very unconvincing they look now. I had to notify Margot to expect to flee at a moment's notice, but I could not write to her directly because of censorship. There was, however, no censorship on a letter I wrote to a friend still in the regiment and not yet demobbed: I enclosed a letter to Margot which he most kindly drove the 20 miles to Wuppertal and delivered into her hands. She sent back the message that she understood and would be ready.

We agreed I would bear all expenses but that Nick and Kay would come down to the Kent coast, and Nick would come to Germany with me. It was now towards the end of May and we decided on the fishing port at Folkestone to find a boat.

We put up at a boarding house, sallied forth to put out enquiries as to who had a small boat for sale, and soon found the brothers Flint. They had an open boat, by the name of Redshank, 18 feet long with a simple sloop rig and an engine fitted midship – not a proper marine engine, but one that did seem to function satisfactorily. We bought it for £150. As Nick said, one could often see the French coast in summer and we expected no difficulty in making the trip.

It was now late May. Nick and I made a trial trip seven miles along the coast to Dover, and turned into the western harbour entrance. Rather too late we noticed, as we passed through the gap in the harbour wall, that the mast of a sunken ship was sticking out of the water in the entrance. We moored to one of the piers and landed: no one took the slightest notice of us, and we felt we could do the same coming back from France.

We returned to Folkstone harbour, and the wind got up. It was to blow for days, and every day we felt it was too choppy for us to set off. We had to occupy the time somehow. Every evening we all went to the cinema: fortunately there were enough cinemas. We beached the boat and painted her bottom with bitumastic between tides. We frequented the Noah's Ark, a tatty cafe patronised by the local fishermen. One day there we asked what time high tide was that night. None of the fishermen knew: I think they just waited inside and drank tea until they looked outside and saw there was enough water.

While we were there a film company were filming for Temptation Harbour. One scene was shot in the Noah's Ark and we heard the director wanted somebody who would dive into the sea from the harbour for a particular scene. Nick and I went up to him on the set and said one of us would jump in, but not dive, but he wasn't having any. It would have been worth £30, a lot of money. He got somebody, because I remember the scene when I saw the film the next year in Nottingham.

On 6th June the weather was still unsuitable, but we decided to take Redshank on a short trip keeping within shelter of the long harbour wall. Half a mile out the engine suddenly spluttered and went off.

Nothing we could do would induce it to restart, and we were steadily drifting on to Cock Point. All we could do was hoist the sails, which we did, and got them up in time to come about before we ran on the rocks. We were then bowling merrily out to sea in a stiff breeze and a choppy sea so we came about and tried to tack back into harbour, which proved impossible against the tide. For some reason Nick decided to gybe her, instead of turning into the wind. He had the helm, and I had the mainsheet, having been instructed to hang on to it and on no account to let it go. Nick knew little about sailing, and I knew nothing. The sail came over with a great bang,

I hung firmly on to the sheet as I had been told to, and water poured over the lee side. It came so fast there was no chance for the boat to recover. She filled and lay on her side, while we all fell into the sea. With vague thoughts of being dragged down by a sinking ship I swam away a few yards, but finding that the boat floated just below the surface I came back and we all took a grip on the rigging. I think she floated while air remained in the forward locker but all the time the heavy engine was dragging her down, and she slowly sank further below the surface. It was all very well applying the cardinal rule to "stay with the boat," but that really only applies to dinghy sailing, where the boat floats.

Had anyone at the harbour seen us go over, threequarters of a mile away? We discussed the matter and recalled there were always old boys leaning against the sea walls and looking out to sea. Our disaster must have been noticed, even though 10 minutes had passed and there was no sign of any boat coming out to our rescue. Nick and I wondered if we could swim to Cock Point, some half a mile away, but were sure Kay could not make it. Then suddenly Kay saw her handkerchief floating past and grabbed it: she waved it, and there was a toot from the siren of the cross-Channel rail ferry lying in harbour. Was it a coincidence or was it a reply to Kay's wave? She waved the handkerchief again and there was another toot.

I hung firmly on to the sheet as I had been told to, and water poured over the lee side. It came so fast there was no chance for the boat to recover. She filled and lay on her side, while we all fell into the sea.

We knew now it was just a matter of treading water and swimming around until someone arrived to pick us up: we had all our clothes on so did not feel the cold. After a few minutes we could see a motor boat shoot out from the harbour towards us, and as it neared we could see it was the brothers Flint. They were much more worried than we were, and in their panic to start their engine had flooded their carburettor: hence the delay.

From down in the water the freeboard seemed very high: they hauled Kay on board first, or course, and pulled her skirt right over her head in doing so. As they did one respectfully said "It's all right, miss, I'm a married man meself." I don't think at that moment Kay was worried about whether she was clothed or naked. Then it was the turn of Nick and myself, and a difficult pull it was too, to get us on board.

Back to the harbour to find a great crowd waiting for us, including police and an ambulance. With great difficulty we persuaded them not to take us all to hospital for a check-up. Having been back to our guest house and changed into dry clothes, we returned to the harbour to find waiting for us a man who started off: "I am from his Majesty's Receiver of Wrecks, and your boat was last reported as a floating wreck..."

Next day we went out with the Flints and dredged for Redshank, without success – whether anyone ever removed her I do not know. We tipped the Flints a tenner for saving us (which I suppose was the equivalent of £100 later) and I resigned myself to the loss of my uninsured boat. Somehow, with her loss, my enthusiasm for Margot faded, and in any case I had no more money to buy another boat.

Next morning the Daily Express had a small paragraph on the front page headlined Wife Clings to Keel. There weren't many amateur sailors in those days, and a rescue was news.

We returned to Lower Fold. I decided the time had come for me to start earning again. Barclays Bank welcomed me back with open arms, and I was working again before my army service ended: on 6 August 1946.

D G Middleton
December 1987

SINKING LOVE HOW THE SEA COOLS PASSIONS

1988 (NOVEMBER)
CHAPTER 20
RETURN TO EGYPT

RETURN TO EGYPT

In November 1988 I spent two weeks in Cairo, where my son was living and working – just about the time of year, in fact, that I visited Cairo in 1940 on a week's leave from Matruh.

I spent five months there at OCTU so we knew it well. I suppose that what struck me most of all was that the old Kasr-el-Nil Barracks, where we did two months of OCTU all-arms training, had been torn down and replaced by the Hilton Hotel. I had much pleasure in sitting over a drink on the very spot where once I had spent hours square-bashing.

The city itself is changed to the extent that dual-carriageways of three and four lanes each side run everywhere, and the density and behaviour of the traffic has to be seen to be believed. If you are on a three-lane road you can be sure there will be four lines of vehicles, all about six inches apart, all hooting, and jockeying for position. To obey traffic lights is literally treated as optional. Never the cleanest of cities, Cairo seems to be one vast construction site, with half-finished buildings and piles of rubble everywhere, and everything covered in dust. Having said that, there are some exciting and attractive buildings, including the new Opera House on Gezira Island, which was recently built and given by the Japanese.

Some will remember the tram ride out to the Pyramids. It is now built up the whole way, and the trams have disappeared. Beyond, off the desert road to Alexandria, lie two whole new industrial cities in the middle of the desert, one called 6th of October City, and one Sadat City. One of the great sightseeing attractions used to be the bazaar which we knew as the Kuski, and is now called Khan Khalili. It is exactly as it always was, a rabbit warren of fascinating alleyways with tiny open-fronted shops – copper work, leather work, filigree jewellery and so on. I couldn't place the Tipperary Club, which used to be run by the wife of Colonel Seely, just off the Ezbekieh Gardens, but the gardens are still there in the city centre, although they look

"Into this cemetery were gathered from the battlefield burial grounds, and from scattered desert graves, many of those who gave their lives during the campaign in Libya. The men who fought and died with them, but have no known grave, are commemorated on the Alamein Memorial which stands in El Alamein War Cemetery."

more like allotments now. At their other end is Opera Square, and the old Opera Casino is still there but now a cinema. It was one of the so-called night clubs which was open to other ranks and was kept by an imposing woman by the name of Madam Badia. Her daughter was the most beautiful belly dancer I have ever seen, and was the great attraction, but she was strictly guarded by the dragon, her mother. Some of us went there from Mens Camp the last evening before going up the desert to Tobruk, and I recall being politely removed from the stage by MPs.

Some will have known the Gezira Club. It is still there, but has a sadly run-down air, although crowded with Egyptians. The pool is empty, and is theoretically under repair, and the Club is now dry too, as befits a Muslim country. Those John Collins at the poolside remain only a memory.

The highlight of the holiday for me was a visit to Alamein Cemetery. Most of those who died at Knightsbridge are buried in Knightsbridge War Cemetery at Acroma, fifteen miles west of Tobruk. To quote the War Graves Commission:

"Into this cemetery were gathered from the battlefield burial grounds, and from scattered desert graves, many of those who gave their lives during the campaign in Libya. The men who fought and died with them, but have no known grave, are commemorated on the Alamein Memorial which stands in El Alamein War Cemetery."

It is rather too far to drive in comfort from Cairo to Alamein and return the same day, so we combined it with a weekend in Alex. The Muslim weekend being Friday and Saturday, we travelled to Alex on Thursday evening, and drove up the desert road to Alamein on Friday 11th November. The road is now dual carriageway the whole way, and by-passes Alamein itself, so it is necessary to divert onto the old road into the village to reach the Allied Cemetery. It lies 65 miles from Alex and about a mile from the sea. Like all British War Cemeteries it is perfectly kept, ordered and peaceful. Although it was 11th November it was empty, but there was to be a service there on Remembrance Sunday, two days later, for a coach party of British residents from Cairo.

We passed first through a gateway and down a path to the cloisters, which constitute the Memorial, and which bear the names of some 5,000 dead who have no known grave. Beyond lie over 7,000 gravestones of Allied Forces. To quote the War Graves Commission again:

> **"They are the graves of men who died at all stages of the desert campaigns, brought in from a wide area round about, but especially those who died in the Battle of El Alamein and in the period immediately before that."**

"They are the graves of men who died at all stages of the desert campaigns, brought in from a wide area round about, but especially those who died in the Battle of El Alamein and in the period immediately before that."

In the pavement is a central stone with the words:

"To the Glory of God and to the undying memory of the Eighth Army, 23rd October – 4th November 1942."

Southward through the graves runs a broad pathway flanked by low purple bougainvillea bushes in full bloom. At the far end with the desert stretching away into the distance, stands a great stone cross with a sword superimposed on it, the point downwards.

I somehow did not expect to find here any mention of the South Notts Hussars who died at Knightsbridge, over 300 miles away. However, while wandering in the cloisters and glancing casually at the thousands of names on the walls, my wife Vivienne's eye was suddenly caught by the words "South Nottinghamshire Hussars".

Below, the first three names were:
   Lieut Colonel Seely, WE
   Bty Sjt Major Lame WA
   Serjeant Bland PSP
   .. then many more.
   Colonel Bill Seely and Pat Bland: Pat, with whom I had shared a tent at Hadera, or was it Gedera? I was taken aback, and much moved, and the years fell away.

We crossed the road for a light lunch at the Alamein Rest House, where an omelette seemed the safest bet (actually it was very good). Next door was the Alamein Museum, with old Italian artillery outside, also tanks, including small arms, maps, charges and portraits of war leaders, including "General WEEVEL" "General OCKNOLIK" and "General DEGOUL".

A few miles further on we reached the German and Italian Memorials. Neither appeared to have a cemetery attached, although the Italian interior walls contained the names of all the dead. Each of the three Memorials seemed to typify the culture of its own country: ours simple and orderly, the German very solid, and the Italian light and graceful.

I gazed out of the desert in which I had lived for so long. Not many people visit Alamein nowadays – the few who visit Egypt on package holidays seldom get the chance – but I feel privileged to have been once more.

D G Middleton

"To the Glory of God and to the undying memory of the Eighth Army, 23rd October – 4th November 1942."

HUSSAR
MAP LEGEND

Countries that Dennis's wartime adventures took him through.

BRITAIN
Nottingham
Redesdale
Malton
Wragby
Southampton
Liverpool
Shoreham
London
York

FRANCE
Marseilles
Calais

PALESTINE*
Haifa
El Mughar
Hadera
Rebovet
Tel Aviv
Jaffa
Jerusalem
Asluj
Beersheba

EGYPT
Alamein
Cairo
Alexandria
Mersa Matruh
Maktilah
Tahag
Sidi Barrani

LIBYA
Tripoli
Tobruk
Tmimi

TUNISIA
Tunis
Le Kef
Goubellat

ALGERIA
Algiers
Sida Moussa
Constantine

MALTA
Valletta

ITALY
Rome
Taranto
Altamura
Ancona
Naples

BELGIUM
Antwerp

GERMANY
Hamburg
Dusseldorf
Essen
Greuenbroich
Neuastenberg

*All places in Palestine were visited before the emergence of Israel.

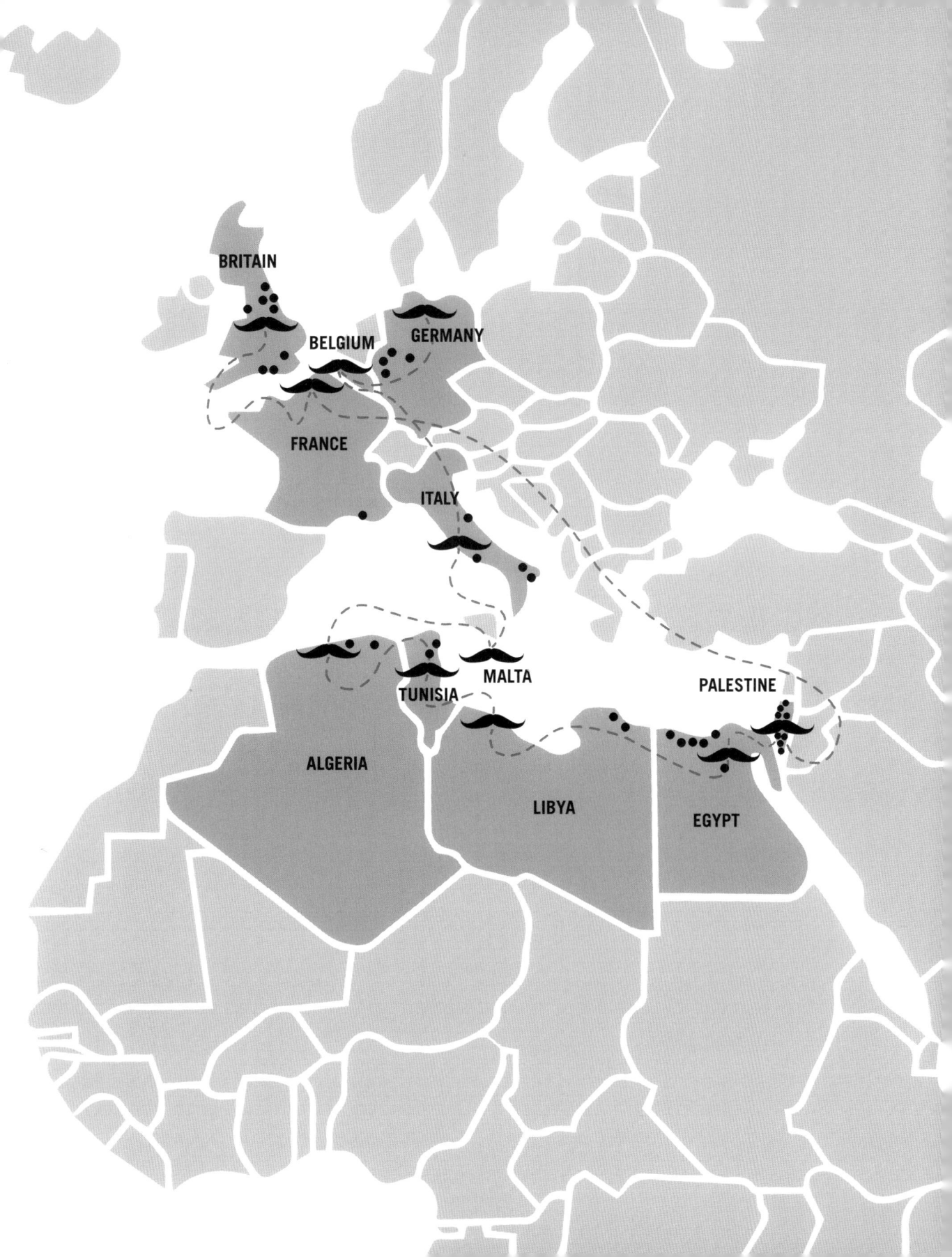

BRITAIN

BELGIUM

GERMANY

FRANCE

ITALY

MALTA

TUNISIA

PALESTINE

ALGERIA

LIBYA

EGYPT

SEVEN GREAT ESCAPES

DGM portrait

DENNIS'S SEVEN GREAT ESCAPES

Dennis left a hand written note listing 7 times he had a narrow escape.

1. Machine guns from German bomber in Tobruk

2. Rifle fire on the wire aimed at DGM

3. Shelling of OP - 20 minutes accurately on DGM's trench

4. Knightsbridge missed

5. Captured and later released

6. Bomb 6ft away on gun position

7. Machine gun at night mending wire in the salient, forward of front line trench

MEMOIRS OF A NOT TOO SERIOUS HUSSAR

1939, The summer of the Breveur. Dennis took a walking holiday in the French Alps in 1939 before the outbreak of war.

MEMOIRS OF A NOT TOO SERIOUS HUSSAR

Above: 1942, OCTU.
Right: 1940, Brameld, Collihole, Bush, Coup

Above: 1942, Cairo, Gillick, Bob, DGM, Jon Sinclair
Above right: 1942, OCTU, Bill Williams
Right: DGM third row and third from right.

MEMOIRS OF A NOT TOO SERIOUS HUSSAR

Above: 1947, Norfolk Broads, Dennis & Peter Middleton

MEMOIRS OF A NOT TOO SERIOUS HUSSAR

Sergeant Vivienne the marker (not the staff sergeant in front). Although they only met after the war, Dennis' future wife Vivienne also did her bit on the home front.

Top and left: 1950, wedding day
Above: 1949, with Vivienne at Prussia cove

MEMOIRS OF A NOT TOO SERIOUS HUSSAR

1992, DGM at Lisbon castle

MEMOIRS OF A NOT TOO SERIOUS HUSSAR

1996, DGM holding his grandson James aged 10 days

Above: The 1939-1945 Star, The Africa Star, The Italy Star, The France & Germany Star, War Medal 1939-1945